The Educator's Guide to Social Media and the Internet Age

Empowering Students with Digital Literacy, Etiquette, and Critical Thinking Skills

"Equipping educators to navigate, teach, and empower students in the digital age."

By Leslie Che

Contents

Introduction: The Digital Shift in Education

Overview of the Digital Transformation of Education

In the past two decades, education has undergone a monumental transformation, driven by the rise of the internet and social media. Classrooms are no longer confined by four walls; learning is now a global, interconnected experience where students can access vast amounts of information instantly. Digital platforms, once considered supplementary to traditional teaching methods, have become central to modern pedagogy. This shift, while empowering, also brings new challenges—both for students who must navigate a complex digital world and for educators who must teach them to do so responsibly.

Technology in Education: A Historical Perspective

The digital transformation of education began with the integration of computers into schools in the late 20th century, primarily to aid research and typing skills. However, with the rise of the internet in the 1990s and the advent of Web 2.0

technologies in the 2000s, the internet shifted from being a source of static information to a dynamic, interactive learning environment. Social media platforms such as Facebook, Twitter, and YouTube transformed communication, allowing for collaborative learning and knowledge-sharing on an unprecedented scale.

From Traditional Classrooms to Digital Ecosystems

Education today is a digital ecosystem. Online platforms, learning management systems (LMS), video conferencing tools, and social media are integral to daily academic operations. Educators now use digital tools like Google Classroom, Moodle, and Zoom to conduct classes, assign projects, and engage with students remotely. The use of multimedia content, such as videos, podcasts, and interactive simulations, has made learning more engaging and accessible, catering to various learning styles.

However, this digital expansion also means that students are constantly exposed to both the benefits and the risks of the internet. Social media platforms, in particular, play a significant role in shaping students' perceptions, interactions, and even academic outcomes. As such, it is no longer sufficient for educators to focus solely on traditional curricula; they must also integrate digital literacy, etiquette, and critical thinking into their teaching strategies to prepare students for the realities of this new world.

Why Educators Need to Address Internet and Social Media Literacy

The Reality of Internet Overload

Today's students are "digital natives" who have grown up with technology, but that doesn't mean they are immune to its dangers. While they are adept at using digital tools, they often lack the critical thinking skills needed to navigate the vast amounts of information they encounter online. Social media, in particular, is a double-edged sword—while it offers platforms for communication, creativity, and collaboration, it also presents numerous challenges, such as misinformation, cyberbullying, data privacy concerns, and the pressures of social validation.

The Dangers of Digital Misinformation and Fake News

One of the most pressing issues in today's digital age is the spread of misinformation. Fake news, clickbait, and biased content are rampant across social media platforms, making it difficult for students to discern fact from fiction. Educators need to equip students with the tools to critically evaluate online content, identify credible sources, and avoid falling prey to manipulation. Failure to address this aspect of internet literacy could result in a generation of misinformed individuals who are unable to make informed decisions based on reliable information.

The Importance of Digital Etiquette

In addition to developing critical thinking skills, educators must emphasize the importance of digital etiquette. Students often treat online interactions casually, forgetting that their words and actions in digital spaces have real-world consequences. Whether it's through text messages, emails, or social media posts, the way individuals communicate online can impact personal relationships, academic performance, and even future career prospects. Teaching students to behave responsibly, respectfully, and ethically online is crucial in preventing issues such as cyberbullying, harassment, and digital footprint mismanagement.

Cyberbullying and the Need for Empathy in Digital Spaces

Cyberbullying is one of the darker aspects of internet and social media use. The anonymity and reach of online platforms make it easier for individuals to engage in harmful behaviour, often without facing immediate consequences. Students must understand the impact of their actions and develop digital empathy—recognizing that their words online can cause real emotional harm. Educators play a critical role in fostering this empathy, teaching students not only the importance of kindness but also how to recognize and intervene in harmful online behaviour.

Purpose of the Book

Equipping Educators for a Digital Age

The primary purpose of this book is to provide educators with the knowledge, tools, and strategies necessary to address the digital realities of the modern world. While students may be adept at using digital devices, they often lack the depth of understanding required to use these tools responsibly and effectively. This book aims to bridge that gap by offering educators a comprehensive guide to teaching digital literacy, etiquette, and critical thinking.

The role of an educator in the internet age goes beyond imparting subject-specific knowledge; it involves preparing students to navigate the complexities of the digital landscape, helping them develop the skills to analyse information critically, communicate responsibly, and engage empathetically with others online.

Key Focus Areas of the Book

1. **Digital Literacy**: Educators will learn how to teach students to critically evaluate digital content, understand the role of algorithms in shaping online experiences, and identify credible sources in an age of rampant misinformation.

2. **Digital Etiquette**: The book emphasizes the importance of teaching students to communicate responsibly and respectfully online, ensuring that they understand the long-term impact of their digital footprint.

3. **Critical Thinking in Digital Spaces**: Developing students' ability to question, analyse, and reflect on the information they encounter online is essential for navigating the complexities of the modern internet.

4. **Empathy and Responsible Online Behaviour**: Educators will be equipped with strategies to foster empathy and kindness in digital interactions, helping students create positive online communities.

A Call to Action for Educators

The internet and social media are here to stay, and their influence on education and society will only continue to grow. As educators, we are responsible for not only adapting to these changes but also for leading the way in teaching the next generation how to use these tools wisely. By focusing on digital literacy, etiquette, and critical thinking, this book empowers educators to foster a generation of informed, responsible, and empathetic digital citizens who are well-prepared for the challenges and opportunities of the digital age.

Chapter 1: Understanding the Digital Landscape

The Evolution of the Internet and Social Media

The internet has evolved at an astonishing pace, from its humble beginnings as a network for academic communication in the 1960s to a global system connecting billions of people today. The internet's first major milestone was the creation of the World Wide Web in 1989 by Tim Berners-Lee, which made it easier for users to access and share information through websites. Initially, the web was a one-way street, with users consuming static content created by a limited number of providers. This era, commonly known as Web 1.0, set the foundation for the information revolution.

With the advent of Web 2.0 in the early 2000s, the internet became more interactive and participatory. Users could now create and share content themselves, leading to the rise of blogs, wikis, and, most significantly, social media platforms. This marked the transition from passive consumption to active participation in the digital realm. Web 2.0 enabled platforms like MySpace and Facebook to emerge, revolutionizing how people interacted online.

Social media platforms quickly became hubs for connection, content creation, and communication, and by the mid-2000s, their influence on social behaviour and cultural norms was undeniable. The concept of the "digital native" emerged to describe individuals who grew up with internet access and naturally integrated digital tools into their everyday lives.

Today, the internet is an essential part of modern society, driving communication, commerce, education, and entertainment. Social media platforms play a particularly critical role in shaping how people interact, learn, and perceive the world around them. The current era, sometimes referred to as Web 3.0, introduces more sophisticated algorithms, artificial intelligence, and personalized experiences, further transforming the digital landscape and amplifying the influence of these platforms.

Major Platforms Shaping Student Behaviour

1. Facebook, launched in 2004, was one of the first social media platforms to achieve global reach. With over 2.8 billion active users, Facebook has transformed how people connect and communicate online. Although its user base is aging, Facebook remains a major player, particularly in developing regions and professional contexts.

For students, Facebook serves as both a social networking site and a source of information. Groups and events allow for collaboration and knowledge sharing, while its algorithm shapes what users see, often influencing their worldviews. However, Facebook has also been criticized for its role in the spread of misinformation and for its addictive nature.

2. Instagram, acquired by Facebook in 2012, is a visually driven platform with over a billion active users. Known for its emphasis on photos and short videos, Instagram significantly shapes student behaviour by promoting a culture of image curation and instant gratification. Filters and "likes" fuel the need for social validation, while influencers set trends that can affect everything from fashion to mental health.

The platform's popularity among younger audiences has made it a key influence on self-perception and body image, with studies showing links between Instagram usage and issues such as anxiety and depression. In educational contexts, however, Instagram can also be used creatively for storytelling, visual projects, and engagement with visual content.

3. TikTok, launched in 2016, has quickly become one of the most influential platforms for younger users, with its short-form videos and algorithmically driven content discovery. TikTok's ability to capture attention and drive viral trends makes it a powerful force in shaping student behaviour, from influencing their consumption of entertainment and news to their social interactions.

TikTok's format encourages quick, engaging content, which can be used effectively in educational contexts to disseminate information and foster creativity. However, its addictive nature and the ease of accessing inappropriate content also pose challenges for educators in managing students' screen time and exposure.

4. Snapchat, launched in 2011, is a multimedia messaging app with a focus on temporary content. Its ephemeral nature encourages quick, informal communication among its users, predominantly teenagers and young adults. Snapchat has redefined the way young people communicate, with its emphasis on quick visuals and messages that disappear after a short time.

For students, Snapchat can foster real-time collaboration and engagement. However, its temporary nature can also lead to impulsive behaviour, with students sometimes posting content without considering long-term consequences. It is also a platform that educators need to address in terms of online safety, privacy, and digital etiquette.

5. YouTube is the world's largest video-sharing platform, and it plays a substantial role in shaping student behaviour. Whether used for entertainment, learning, or self-expression, YouTube offers vast resources for students to consume and create content. Educational channels, tutorials, and lectures make YouTube a valuable tool for learning, but the platform also exposes students to misinformation, extremist content, and unhealthy social comparison.

The comment sections on YouTube videos are often filled with toxic behaviour, highlighting the need for educators to teach students about digital etiquette and the importance of constructive engagement online.

The Role of Technology in Transforming Educational Settings

Technology has not only transformed how students behave online but has also fundamentally altered the structure and delivery of education. The traditional classroom model, characterized by face-to-face interaction and paper-based materials, has been expanded by digital tools that enable more flexible, engaging, and personalized learning experiences. The following are key areas where technology has revolutionized education:

1. E-Learning Platforms

Learning management systems (LMS) like Google Classroom, Moodle, and Blackboard have made it easier for educators to manage content, track student progress, and provide feedback. These platforms allow for asynchronous learning, enabling students to access resources and complete assignments at their own pace. This flexibility has been particularly beneficial in higher education and during periods of remote learning, such as the COVID-19 pandemic.

2. Multimedia Content

Technology has made it possible for educators to integrate multimedia content into their lessons, enhancing engagement and catering to different learning styles. Video lectures, podcasts, and interactive simulations allow for more dynamic and accessible education. Students can access content in multiple formats, helping them retain information more effectively. Platforms like YouTube and educational apps have democratized learning by making high-quality resources available to anyone with internet access.

3. Gamification and Interactive Learning

Gamification is another major trend in education, leveraging game mechanics to make learning more engaging and fun. Platforms like Kahoot!, Quizlet, and Duolingo use points, leaderboards, and rewards to motivate students, particularly in subjects that require repetition and practice. Virtual reality (VR) and augmented reality (AR) are also being integrated into classrooms, allowing students to explore virtual worlds, conduct virtual experiments, and visualize complex concepts in an immersive way.

4. Personalized Learning through AI and Data Analytics

Artificial intelligence (AI) and data analytics are increasingly being used to personalize education. Adaptive learning platforms analyse student data to adjust the pace and content of lessons to meet individual needs. This approach ensures that each student is challenged appropriately, addressing gaps in knowledge while promoting mastery of subjects. AI-driven tutoring systems provide real-time feedback and support, offering students personalized guidance outside the classroom.

5. Social Media as a Learning Tool

Social media platforms are not just distractions—they can also serve as powerful educational tools. Facebook groups, Twitter chats, and LinkedIn discussions allow students and educators to collaborate, share resources, and engage in professional development. Hashtags, blogs, and wikis enable peer-to-peer learning and crowd-sourced knowledge building. Social media can help students develop digital literacy skills, as they must critically assess the information they encounter in these spaces.

Challenges in the Digital Education Era

While the benefits of technology in education are evident, challenges remain. The digital divide continues to prevent equitable access to technology and high-speed internet, particularly in underserved communities. Furthermore, the over-reliance on technology can lead to reduced face-to-face communication skills, shorter attention spans, and issues related to screen addiction. These challenges must be addressed through thoughtful educational policies, targeted interventions, and ongoing training for educators.

Conclusion

Understanding the digital landscape is critical for educators who must guide students through an increasingly complex world of online interactions. The rapid evolution of social media platforms has fundamentally shaped student behaviour, necessitating the integration of digital literacy, etiquette, and critical thinking into educational curricula. As education continues to transform, educators must remain adaptable, continuously learning about the tools and platforms that shape their students' lives. By doing so, they can better equip students with the skills they need to thrive in the digital age.

Defining Digital Literacy: More than Just Knowing How to Use Devices

Digital literacy, at its core, extends far beyond the mere ability to use computers, smartphones, and other devices. While knowing how to navigate digital tools is an essential component, true digital literacy encompasses a deeper understanding of the digital world and the ability to critically engage with the information it presents.

In essence, digital literacy includes the capacity to locate, evaluate, and effectively use information in digital environments. This means not only being familiar with the basic functionalities of technology but also possessing the critical thinking skills necessary to assess the credibility, reliability, and bias of online content. Moreover, it involves understanding digital communication norms, privacy concerns, cybersecurity, and ethical behaviour online.

Key Components of Digital Literacy

1. **Technical Skills**: Basic competencies like typing, navigating the internet, using email, and interacting with various apps and platforms.

2. **Information Literacy**: The ability to research, analyse, and verify online information, distinguishing between credible sources and misinformation.

3. **Critical Thinking**: The practice of questioning and challenging the content encountered online, rather than passively accepting it.

4. **Digital Communication Skills**: Understanding the nuances of online communication, including etiquette, tone, and the responsible use of social media.

5. **Cybersecurity Awareness**: Recognising the importance of safeguarding personal data, understanding online risks, and employing safe online practices.

6. **Ethical Use of Digital Tools**: Being conscious of digital footprints, respecting intellectual property, and engaging in fair online behaviour.

For educators, imparting these skills to students is vital. In today's world, students not only need to know how to operate devices but must also understand how to navigate the complexities of the internet safely, responsibly, and thoughtfully. Without these skills, they risk falling prey to misinformation, manipulation, and other online dangers.

Understanding Online Information Ecosystems and Critical Thinking

The internet is an expansive ecosystem where information flows freely and rapidly, but not all content is equal in terms of credibility or value. Educators must guide students in understanding how the online information ecosystem works and the mechanisms behind the spread of information.

The speed and accessibility of the internet mean that anyone, from professional journalists to everyday individuals, can produce and disseminate content. Social media platforms and search engines further complicate matters, as they often prioritise engagement-driven content, regardless of its factual accuracy. This can lead to echo chambers, where users are exposed to biased information that reinforces their existing beliefs.

Types of Online Information

- **News and Journalism**: Traditionally vetted and researched content produced by reputable news outlets.

- **User-Generated Content**: Blogs, social media posts, and forums, which may range from personal opinions to well-researched analyses.

- **Advertisements**: Often disguised as genuine content, these promote products or services.

- **Misinformation and Disinformation**: Inaccurate or misleading information spread either accidentally (misinformation) or deliberately (disinformation).

Educators need to teach students how to navigate these different sources of information by developing their critical thinking skills. Critical thinking is essential in identifying credible information and distinguishing between fact and fiction. Students should be taught to ask questions such as:

- Who created this content, and what is their purpose?

- What sources are cited, if any, and are they credible?

- Is the information being presented objectively, or does it seem to have a bias?

- How does this piece of information fit into the larger context of the topic being discussed?

Developing critical thinking ensures that students become active, questioning participants in the digital world, rather than passive consumers of content.

How to Teach Students to Assess Credibility, Bias, and Accuracy of Online Content

Given the sheer volume of online content, students must be equipped with the tools to evaluate its credibility, bias, and accuracy. This is one of the most challenging yet essential aspects of digital literacy. Below are practical methods and strategies for teaching students these crucial evaluation skills.

1. Source Evaluation Frameworks - One widely used method for teaching students how to assess credibility is the CRAAP test, which stands for **Currency, Relevance, Authority, Accuracy**, and **Purpose**. This framework encourages students to evaluate:

- **Currency**: Is the information up to date? Is it still relevant to the topic or has it been superseded by more recent findings?

- **Relevance**: Is the information relevant to the question at hand? Does it address the topic comprehensively or only superficially?

- **Authority**: Who is the author or publisher? Are they qualified to speak on the subject? Are they associated with a reputable institution?

- **Accuracy**: Can the information be verified through other credible sources? Does it cite reputable references?

- **Purpose**: Is the content intended to inform, persuade, entertain, or sell something? Does it appear objective or biased?

Teaching students to apply this framework allows them to critically engage with content and make informed decisions about its reliability.

2. Recognising Bias - Bias in online content can be subtle or overt. Educators should teach students how to identify bias in language, argumentation, and source selection. Encourage students to ask:

- Is the author presenting all sides of the argument?

- Are emotive or exaggerated words being used to persuade the reader?

- Does the source come from a particular political, cultural, or commercial standpoint that could affect its objectivity?

One effective exercise is to present students with two articles on the same topic from different perspectives and have them compare the language and arguments used. This helps students recognise how bias can shape the presentation of information.

3. Cross-Referencing Information - One of the simplest ways to verify accuracy is to cross-check the information against multiple sources. Encourage students to consult a range of credible outlets and compare their findings. This not only verifies the information but exposes students to multiple viewpoints, fostering more balanced understanding.

4. Fact-Checking Tools - Educators should introduce students to professional fact-checking tools and websites, such as **Snopes, FactCheck.org,** and the **BBC Reality Check**. These platforms specialise in debunking misinformation and providing evidence-based assessments of viral content.

Additionally, browser extensions like **NewsGuard** and **Media Bias/Fact Check** offer real-time assessments of the credibility and bias of websites students may visit. Integrating these tools into classroom activities ensures students become familiar with reliable resources.

5. Practical Classroom Activities

- **Debate**: Create classroom debates on topical issues where students must research their stance and provide evidence from credible sources. This encourages the application of critical thinking and source evaluation.

- **Fact-Checking Assignments**: Provide students with a piece of online content—perhaps a viral social media post or a controversial news story— and ask them to investigate its accuracy and bias.

- **Media Comparison Projects**: Assign students the task of analysing the coverage of a single news event across various platforms (e.g., BBC, The Guardian, social media). Students can compare how different outlets present the story, considering bias and accuracy.

Conclusion

In an era where information is abundant and not always reliable, digital literacy must be a priority for educators. Teaching students to think critically about the digital content they consume, and to evaluate it for credibility, bias, and accuracy, is essential to developing responsible and informed digital citizens. By equipping students with these skills, educators empower them to navigate the complexities of the online world with discernment and confidence.

Chapter 3: Social Media Etiquette in the Classroom

The Importance of Online Manners, Respect, and Responsibility

As the digital classroom becomes more prominent in today's educational landscape, the need for social media etiquette in academic environments has never been greater. Social media platforms and other online communication tools have blurred the lines between personal and academic spaces, making it essential for students to understand the expectations of appropriate behaviour in both contexts.

Online manners, often referred to as *netiquette*, are the standards of politeness and respect that should govern all online interactions. When students participate in academic discussions through platforms like Google Classroom, Zoom, or social media, these manners shape the quality of communication and set the tone for respectful engagement.

Respectful online behaviour encompasses a range of actions:

- **Respect for others' opinions**: Whether on social media or academic forums, it is important for students to engage with differing perspectives thoughtfully and courteously. Disagreements should be managed diplomatically, avoiding inflammatory language or personal attacks.

- **Maintaining privacy and confidentiality**: Students must be aware that what is shared online can have lasting consequences. Sensitive information, whether personal or academic, should never be disclosed without permission.

- **Timeliness and attentiveness**: In digital communication, responding in a timely and engaged manner demonstrates respect for others' time and contributions.

Responsibility online means recognising the impact one's words and actions can have in a digital space. Unlike face-to-face communication, digital interactions often lack immediate cues such as body language or tone, increasing the potential for miscommunication. Students must be taught that digital responsibility includes thinking before posting, understanding the potential reach of their words, and upholding a standard of accountability for their actions online.

Educators must emphasise that poor online etiquette can result in:

- Damaged relationships or misunderstandings between peers.

- Disciplinary action from schools or universities for breaches of conduct.

- Long-term repercussions on a student's digital footprint, including effects on future employability or reputation.

By instilling good online manners, educators are not only fostering a positive classroom environment but also preparing students for their future roles as responsible digital citizens in both personal and professional contexts.

Teaching Students to Understand Tone and Context in Digital Communication

One of the biggest challenges in digital communication is the absence of non-verbal cues like facial expressions, tone of voice, and body language. These are vital elements in face-to-face interactions that help convey meaning and emotion. When students communicate digitally—whether via email, chat, or social media posts— this lack of context can lead to misunderstandings or unintended offence.

Tone in digital messages can be easily misinterpreted. For example, a straightforward statement may be perceived as curt or rude, while humour or sarcasm may be misunderstood as seriousness. It is important to teach students how to adjust their digital tone and how to interpret others' tones accurately.

Strategies for Teaching Digital Tone and Context:

1. **Use of Emojis and Punctuation**: While it is essential for students to maintain a professional tone in academic settings, they should also understand how symbols like emojis or punctuation can soften or clarify a message. For example, adding an emoji to indicate humour can prevent misinterpretation of tone.

2. **Choosing the Right Words**: In digital spaces, words matter even more. Educators should encourage students to take extra care when crafting their messages, thinking about how their words may be received without the benefit of voice inflections or physical presence. Polite phrases like "please," "thank you," and "I appreciate your thoughts" can go a long way in preventing miscommunication.

3. **Clarification and Follow-Up**: If students feel that their message might be unclear, they should learn to follow up with a clarification. Phrases like, "Just to clarify…" or "I hope this message came across clearly" can smooth over potential misunderstandings.

4. **Context-Sensitivity**: Students should be taught to tailor their messages according to the platform they are using. What may be appropriate in a personal text message or social media chat might not be suitable in an academic email or discussion post. Knowing the context of the communication—whether formal, informal, personal, or academic—is key to determining the appropriate tone.

5. **Pausing Before Posting**: Encourage students to take a moment before sending messages to consider how the recipient might interpret their words. In fast-paced social media environments, it can be easy to post without thinking through the implications, leading to impulsive comments or posts that can cause offence.

6. **Learning from Mistakes**: Misunderstandings in digital communication are inevitable, but they provide important learning moments. Teaching students how to handle misunderstandings gracefully—through apologies, clarifications, or direct communication—can help resolve conflicts quickly and maintain positive relationships.

Examples of Good and Poor Digital Etiquette in Personal and Academic Settings

Understanding what constitutes good and bad online behaviour is essential for teaching students how to conduct themselves in digital spaces. Below are examples of both positive and negative online etiquette in personal and academic settings.

Good Digital Etiquette Examples:

- **Academic Emailing**: A student reaches out to a lecturer with a respectful and clear email:

  "Dear Professor Smith,

  I hope this message finds you well. I would like to request clarification on the homework assignment for next week. Could you please confirm the submission guidelines?

  Thank you for your assistance.

  Best regards,

  Jane Doe."

- **Respectful Social Media Engagement**: During an online classroom discussion on social media, a student expresses disagreement with a classmate's opinion in a polite and thoughtful manner:

  "I understand your perspective on this issue, and you raise some interesting points. However, I feel that the data we reviewed last week suggests a different outcome. I'd love to hear your thoughts on that."

- **Acknowledging Others' Contributions**: In a group chat or discussion board, a student acknowledges and builds upon a peer's idea rather than ignoring or dismissing it:

  "I think what John said about the importance of context in digital communication is really relevant. I'd like to add that tone is also crucial, especially when we're interacting with people from different cultural backgrounds."

Poor Digital Etiquette Examples:

- **Aggressive Responses in Online Forums**: During an academic debate, a student lashes out at a peer's opinion:

  "That's completely ridiculous! You obviously don't know what you're talking about!"

- **Ignoring Proper Email Etiquette**: A student sends a brief, demanding email to their lecturer without proper structure or respect:

  "Need you to resend the assignment file. Can't find it."

- **Posting Without Thought**: A student makes an inappropriate comment on social media during a group project discussion:

  "This project is a total waste of time. Why do we even bother?"

These examples highlight the significant impact of tone, structure, and thoughtfulness in digital interactions. Poor digital etiquette can result in strained relationships, academic repercussions, or misunderstandings, while good etiquette fosters collaboration, respect, and clear communication.

Conclusion

Social media and digital communication tools are integral to modern education. By instilling proper social media etiquette in the classroom, educators can equip students with the skills needed for respectful and responsible online interactions. From understanding tone and context to demonstrating respect for others' opinions, digital etiquette is crucial in both personal and academic settings. With these skills, students will not only navigate the academic digital world successfully but also develop into conscientious and thoughtful digital citizens.

Chapter 4: Privacy and Security in the Digital Age

Understanding Privacy Settings and Data Protection

In today's digital world, privacy and security have become paramount concerns for individuals, institutions, and governments alike. As students become more integrated into online spaces through social media, educational platforms, and digital tools, understanding how to safeguard personal data is critical. Educators play a crucial role in guiding students to navigate these spaces securely.

Privacy settings are the first line of defence for users when interacting with various online platforms. Whether it's social media, email services, or cloud storage systems, each platform provides privacy settings that allow users to control who can see their content, what data is collected, and how that data is used. Unfortunately, many students and even adults do not fully understand the implications of leaving these settings unchecked.

Key Elements of Privacy Settings:

- **Account Visibility:** On social media platforms like Facebook, Instagram, and TikTok, students should know how to control who sees their posts. Public profiles may expose personal information to a wide audience, including potential online predators or data harvesters. Educators can teach students how to make their accounts private, only allowing friends or approved contacts to view their content.

- **Data Sharing and Tracking:** Many apps and websites track user activity and share data with third parties, often for advertising purposes. Students need to be aware of these practices and should be encouraged to limit data sharing. For example, turning off location tracking on social apps or opting out of personalised ads can reduce the amount of data they unwittingly share.

- **Password Protection:** Strong, unique passwords are essential for protecting online accounts. A password should ideally include a combination of uppercase and lowercase letters, numbers, and special characters. Educators should stress the importance of not using the same password across multiple platforms and consider introducing students to password managers as a secure method for managing multiple credentials.

Data protection laws, such as the **UK's Data Protection Act 2018** and **GDPR (General Data Protection Regulation)**, govern how personal information must be handled. These regulations enforce strict rules on organisations regarding data privacy, and students should be made aware of their rights under these laws. They should understand that companies are obligated to secure their data and must inform them of any data breaches that could expose their personal information.

How Educators Can Teach Students to Safeguard Their Personal Data

Educators have the unique opportunity to influence how students view and protect their personal data online. By incorporating privacy and security lessons into the curriculum, students can develop habits that will serve them well both in their academic and personal lives.

Strategies for Teaching Data Protection:

1. **Practical Workshops on Privacy Settings**: Educators can conduct hands-on sessions where students review and adjust their privacy settings on various platforms. This might include setting up two-factor authentication (2FA), creating strong passwords, and reviewing what information apps are tracking.

2. **Case Studies on Data Breaches**: Real-world examples of data breaches, such as the Facebook-Cambridge Analytica scandal or large-scale breaches affecting companies like Equifax, can help illustrate the importance of data protection. Discussions around how these breaches occurred, their consequences, and how they could have been prevented will make the concept of data security more relatable.

3. **Encouraging Regular Data Audits**: Students should be taught to conduct regular audits of their online presence. This could involve reviewing app permissions, deleting unused accounts, and purging old social media posts. Educators can provide students with checklists to help them systematically safeguard their data.

4. **Introducing Encryption**: Though encryption is often seen as a technical concept, it can be explained in simple terms. Educators should ensure students understand how encryption protects their data, especially on messaging apps such as WhatsApp, which use end-to-end encryption.

5. **Digital Footprint Awareness**: Educators should raise awareness about the long-term consequences of one's digital footprint. What students post online today could potentially be accessible years from now, affecting their personal or professional lives. Lessons should focus on making informed decisions about what is shared online.

Awareness of Cyber Threats, Phishing, and Online Predators

In addition to understanding privacy settings and data protection, students must be aware of the various cyber threats they face while navigating the digital world. From phishing attacks to online predators, the internet presents many risks that can have real-world consequences.

Cyber Threats:

- **Phishing**: Phishing is one of the most common and dangerous cyber threats, involving malicious actors attempting to steal personal information by pretending to be trustworthy entities. Phishing attacks often come in the form of emails, texts, or social media messages that prompt users to click on a link or provide sensitive information.

Educators can train students to recognise the signs of phishing, such as:

  - Suspicious email addresses or domains.

  - Urgent requests for personal information or payment.

  - Misspellings or grammatical errors in messages.

  - Unexpected attachments or links.

Teaching students to verify the legitimacy of messages—by contacting the organisation directly or checking official sources—can prevent them from falling victim to these schemes.

- **Malware and Ransomware**: Malware (malicious software) can infect devices through downloads or compromised websites. Ransomware is a type of malware that locks users out of their systems until a ransom is paid. Students should understand the risks of downloading unknown files or apps and the importance of using up-to-date antivirus software.

- **Social Engineering**: Social engineering exploits human psychology to gain access to information. Students should be taught to be sceptical of strangers asking for personal details, even on seemingly harmless platforms, such as gaming chat rooms or social media.

Online Predators: While social media platforms offer incredible opportunities for connection, they also present dangers in the form of online predators. Students, particularly younger ones, need to be aware of the risks of interacting with strangers online. Educators should address:

- **Grooming**: Predators often build trust over time, slowly collecting personal information from their victims. Students should be taught to recognise the warning signs of grooming, including someone trying to form an inappropriate emotional connection, asking for personal details, or wanting to meet in person.

- **Catfishing**: This refers to the practice of someone creating a fake identity to deceive others. Students should be sceptical of online relationships that seem too good to be true or involve individuals they haven't met in real life.

Educators should create an open dialogue about online dangers and provide students with clear guidance on what to do if they encounter suspicious behaviour or feel uncomfortable during any online interaction.

Best Practices for Staying Safe Online:

- **Do not share personal information** such as home addresses, phone numbers, or financial details with strangers or on public forums.

- **Never meet someone from the internet in person** without a trusted adult's approval and supervision.

- **Report suspicious behaviour** immediately to a teacher, parent, or platform administrator.

- **Block and ignore** unsolicited messages from unknown individuals.

Conclusion

The digital age offers vast opportunities for learning and connection, but it also presents challenges in terms of privacy, security, and safety. As educators, the responsibility to equip students with the skills necessary to protect themselves online is crucial. By fostering an understanding of privacy settings, teaching the importance of personal data protection, and raising awareness about cyber threats, educators can empower students to navigate the internet confidently and securely.

In the next chapter, we will delve into how digital citizenship can be nurtured, focusing on creating respectful, responsible, and informed online participants.

Chapter 5: Nurturing Digital Citizenship in the Classroom

Defining Digital Citizenship: What It Means to Be a Responsible Digital Citizen

As the internet continues to shape how we live, work, and learn, it has become increasingly important to foster a sense of **digital citizenship** among students. Digital citizenship refers to the responsible and ethical use of technology, encouraging users to engage in positive, productive, and respectful online behaviour. In an age where our personal and professional lives are intertwined with digital interactions, educators play a pivotal role in teaching students to navigate these spaces thoughtfully.

A **responsible digital citizen**:

- Understands their rights and responsibilities online.

- Respects others' privacy, opinions, and intellectual property.

- Engages in constructive communication.

- Thinks critically about the content they create, share, or consume.

- Is aware of their digital footprint and its long-term consequences.

Digital citizenship extends beyond just safe online practices—it involves understanding the impact of one's actions in the broader digital community. Students need to recognise that their digital behaviour contributes to a global network of interactions, and their actions online have far-reaching consequences.

Key Elements of Digital Citizenship

There are several core pillars that define good digital citizenship. Educators should integrate these into their teaching to help students develop a comprehensive understanding of how to be responsible digital citizens.

1. **Digital Etiquette**: Respectful communication is crucial in the online world. This includes proper language use, being considerate of others' opinions, and avoiding harmful or inappropriate comments. Encouraging students to pause before posting and think about the impact of their words can significantly reduce harmful online behaviours such as trolling or cyberbullying.

2. **Digital Literacy**: Teaching students how to critically evaluate information they come across online—whether it's articles, videos, or social media posts—is essential. Understanding how to identify misinformation, spot bias, and cross-check sources can protect them from manipulation and help them become more informed participants in digital spaces.

3. **Digital Rights and Responsibilities**: Students should be taught their rights in the digital world, including the right to privacy and free expression. However, they also need to understand that these rights come with responsibilities, such as not infringing on the rights of others and following community guidelines on various platforms.

4. **Online Safety and Security**: Protecting personal data, using strong passwords, and avoiding risky online behaviours are critical aspects of

digital citizenship. Teaching students how to safeguard their privacy and avoid falling victim to scams or cyber threats is crucial for long-term online safety.

5. **Digital Health and Wellness**: Excessive screen time, cyberbullying, and exposure to inappropriate content can negatively impact students' mental health. Educators should teach students about the importance of setting boundaries, managing screen time, and seeking help when they encounter negative online experiences.

6. **Digital Footprint**: Every online interaction leaves a trace that contributes to a person's digital identity. Students need to understand how their digital footprint can affect their reputation, both now and in the future, including their academic and professional prospects. Educators can guide students in making conscious choices about the content they post and share.

How to Teach Digital Citizenship in the Classroom

Teaching digital citizenship is not a one-time lesson but an ongoing process that should be woven into various aspects of education. Here are some strategies for integrating digital citizenship into the curriculum:

1. **Incorporate Digital Citizenship into Existing Subjects**: Digital citizenship lessons don't have to be standalone—they can be integrated into subjects like English, history, or social studies. For example, while teaching a literature class, educators can prompt discussions about how characters

would behave in an online context, drawing parallels to students' digital interactions.

2. **Create Role-Playing Scenarios**: One effective method for teaching digital citizenship is through role-playing. Students can take on different personas and navigate fictional online scenarios. These could include handling negative comments on social media, identifying phishing attempts, or making ethical decisions about sharing content. This hands-on approach helps students think critically about their actions.

3. **Promote Student-Led Discussions**: Encouraging students to lead discussions on issues like cyberbullying, privacy, or online ethics fosters deeper engagement. It gives students a sense of ownership over their learning and allows them to hear diverse perspectives from their peers.

4. **Use Technology for Good**: Assign projects where students use digital tools to create positive online content, such as promoting mental health awareness or creating campaigns to combat cyberbullying. This gives students practical experience in being constructive digital citizens.

5. **Digital Citizenship Pledges**: Have students create their own personal digital citizenship pledges, outlining how they will behave online. This can be a powerful exercise in self-reflection and accountability. These pledges can also serve as a class contract to ensure respectful online interaction throughout the academic year.

6. **Involve Parents and Guardians**: Educators should work closely with families to reinforce digital citizenship at home. Parent-teacher meetings can include discussions on how parents can monitor and guide their children's online activities. Sharing resources with parents—such as guides on setting up parental controls or managing screen time—ensures students receive consistent messaging about responsible digital behaviour.

Case Studies in Digital Citizenship

To further enrich students' understanding, educators can present case studies that illustrate both positive and negative examples of digital citizenship. For example:

- **Positive Example**: An online community where students collaborate to solve problems, share resources, and provide support to each other in a constructive manner. This highlights the power of the internet to foster collaboration and learning.

- **Negative Example**: A case of online harassment, where a student faced cyberbullying after expressing an unpopular opinion on social media. Discussing the impact of cyberbullying and the importance of standing up against harmful behaviours reinforces the need for empathy and respect online.

These case studies can spark discussions about what constitutes good or poor digital citizenship and help students see real-world implications of their online choices.

Why Digital Citizenship Matters in Education

In a world where much of students' social, academic, and professional interactions happen online, the need for **digital citizenship education** has never been more pressing. By nurturing responsible digital citizens, educators are not only preparing students to protect themselves in the digital age but also equipping them to contribute positively to online communities. The skills students develop as digital citizens will carry over into their future careers, relationships, and societal roles.

Digital citizenship education is a critical component of modern learning environments, promoting respect, responsibility, and critical thinking in digital interactions. With technology's ever-growing presence in both personal and professional spheres, educators have the opportunity to shape the next generation of responsible, thoughtful digital participants.

Conclusion

In fostering digital citizenship, educators empower students to navigate the internet with confidence, respect, and integrity. By teaching them the key elements of digital citizenship—such as etiquette, literacy, safety, and wellness—teachers can prepare their students to make thoughtful and ethical decisions online. As the internet continues to evolve, the importance of these lessons will only grow, making digital citizenship a cornerstone of modern education.

In the next chapter, we will examine the power of **digital empathy** and its essential role in creating more meaningful and positive online interactions.

Chapter 6: Teaching Digital Empathy in Educational Settings

What is Digital Empathy?

Digital empathy refers to the ability to understand and share the feelings of others within online environments. It involves recognising the emotional cues of others, even when body language, tone, and facial expressions are absent - making it a more nuanced form of empathy. Given the increasing time spent online, digital empathy has become an essential skill to develop in students to promote meaningful, respectful, and supportive interactions in digital spaces.

In a world where tone and context are often misinterpreted, the ability to be empathetic in online communication can prevent conflicts, reduce toxic behaviour, and foster positive engagement.

The Importance of Digital Empathy in Online Interactions

The absence of face-to-face communication in online spaces increases the likelihood of misunderstandings, as social and emotional cues are harder to detect. This gap can result in:

- **Misinterpretations**: A comment intended as humour may be taken as rude or hostile.

- **Hurtful interactions**: Without real-time feedback, people may post or comment without fully considering the emotional impact on the recipient.

- **Toxicity**: The anonymity of the internet often emboldens individuals to engage in trolling, cyberbullying, or other forms of harmful behaviour without considering the effects on others.

By teaching digital empathy, educators can help students understand how their words and actions impact others and encourage more thoughtful communication.

The Role of Digital Empathy in Preventing Harm

Digital empathy plays a crucial role in:

- **Reducing cyberbullying**: Empathetic individuals are less likely to engage in hurtful behaviour, and more likely to support those who are being bullied.

- **Promoting inclusivity**: Understanding the experiences of others helps build more inclusive online communities, where diverse voices are respected and valued.

- **Improving digital collaboration**: In online learning or work environments, digital empathy facilitates more effective communication and teamwork, as participants are better able to understand each other's needs and viewpoints.

Challenges of Teaching Digital Empathy

Teaching empathy in the digital age presents unique challenges:

- **Lack of visual or auditory cues**: Without tone, body language, or facial expressions, students may struggle to pick up on others' emotions, making it harder to foster empathy.

- **Cultural differences**: Online platforms are global spaces, and different cultural norms around communication can complicate efforts to interpret tone or intention.

- **Instantaneous nature of communication**: The speed of digital interactions often encourages quick, impulsive responses, which may not be well-considered or empathetic.

Educators must guide students through these challenges, offering strategies to ensure that empathy is not lost in digital communication.

Strategies for Teaching Digital Empathy

1. **Encourage Reflection Before Posting** Educators should teach students to take a moment before responding to digital communications. By encouraging students to ask themselves questions like, "How would I feel if I received this message?" or "Could my words be misinterpreted?", they can begin to develop an awareness of the impact of their communication.

2. **Teach Active Listening and Thoughtful Responses** In digital settings, **active listening** involves reading carefully and fully considering someone's perspective before responding. Encouraging students to **acknowledge** the

emotions behind a message (e.g., "I can understand why you feel that way") can help foster more meaningful online interactions.

3. **Role-Playing Scenarios** Role-playing can help students experience how their words might be perceived by others in a digital environment. For example, students could simulate an online group discussion, with some participants tasked with making thoughtful contributions and others playing the role of a disinterested or negative participant. Reflecting on the emotional responses these roles generate can help students understand the importance of empathetic communication.

4. **Create Empathy-Building Projects** Encourage students to engage in online projects that promote **positive social impact**. For example, students could create social media campaigns supporting mental health, combating cyberbullying, or encouraging kindness online. These projects give students hands-on experience in practising digital empathy, while also contributing to a broader online culture of empathy.

5. **Use Technology Tools for Empathy** There are various digital tools that help teach and enhance empathy. For instance, virtual reality (VR) simulations can immerse students in the lives of others, helping them to experience different perspectives. Additionally, some social platforms use AI to detect and alert users to potentially harmful language before it is posted, giving students a moment to reconsider their words.

The Role of Educators in Modelling Digital Empathy

Teachers are role models in both physical and virtual classrooms. By **demonstrating digital empathy** in their own online interactions—whether in email correspondence, class discussions, or feedback—educators can set a powerful example for students.

Best practices for educators include:

- Using inclusive, respectful language in all communications.

- Offering constructive criticism in a thoughtful and considerate manner.

- Being open to feedback from students and demonstrating active listening in online discussions.

Empathy in Digital Group Work and Collaborative Learning

Group work is increasingly conducted through digital platforms. Educators can foster empathy by:

- Encouraging students to appreciate the strengths and contributions of others.

- Promoting positive group dynamics through cooperative tasks, where students are tasked with solving problems collaboratively, considering each other's perspectives, and engaging in open dialogue.

Assessments can also be structured to reward **collaboration** and **supportive behaviours**. This helps shift students' focus from competition to cooperation, reinforcing the importance of empathetic engagement.

Case Studies of Digital Empathy in Online Communities

1. **Support Networks on Social Media**: Online communities centred around mental health support are often excellent examples of digital empathy in action. These groups offer validation, understanding, and advice to individuals struggling with mental health issues, fostering a supportive online environment.

2. **Positive School Environments**: Schools that have integrated digital empathy training into their curriculum often report reduced instances of cyberbullying and an improvement in overall online behaviour. For example, a school that implemented empathy exercises during online group projects saw an increase in respectful communication and collaboration among students.

Why Digital Empathy Matters for the Future

As online communication becomes even more prevalent, the ability to understand and connect with others in digital spaces will be an essential life skill. By cultivating digital empathy, students can:

- Build stronger, more meaningful online relationships.

- Contribute to healthier, more inclusive digital communities.

- Become proactive in creating supportive environments, both online and offline.

In today's globalised, interconnected world, digital empathy also plays a role in promoting **cross-cultural understanding**. The ability to appreciate and respect differences while engaging online helps break down cultural barriers and fosters a more harmonious global digital society.

Conclusion

Teaching digital empathy is not just about preventing harm—it's about empowering students to create positive, constructive digital environments. By understanding the importance of empathy in online communication and equipping students with practical strategies for its application, educators can nurture a generation of thoughtful, compassionate digital citizens.

In the next chapter, we will delve into **cyber safety** and the pivotal role educators play in equipping students to navigate the digital world securely and responsibly.

Chapter 7: Cyber Safety and Responsible Online Behaviour

The Growing Importance of Cyber Safety in Education

In today's interconnected world, the internet offers vast opportunities for learning, communication, and collaboration, but it also comes with significant risks. As students increasingly rely on digital platforms for both personal and academic activities, **cyber safety** has become a critical area of focus for educators. Cyber threats—ranging from data breaches to identity theft, cyberbullying, and phishing scams—are a growing concern. Therefore, educating students about **safe online practices** is essential for their protection and digital wellbeing.

Cyber safety refers to the practice of protecting internet users from the potential risks they may encounter online, including threats to their personal data, privacy, and digital identity. This chapter will explore how educators can teach students to navigate the digital landscape securely and responsibly.

Understanding the Cyber Threat Landscape

Before diving into safety strategies, it's essential to understand the types of threats students may encounter online:

1. **Phishing Scams**: Phishing involves fraudulent attempts to acquire sensitive information (such as passwords or credit card details) by disguising as a trustworthy entity. Students need to recognise suspicious emails, links, and messages designed to steal personal information.

2. **Malware and Viruses**: Malware, including viruses, spyware, and ransomware, can infect devices and compromise security. Students should be taught how to avoid downloading malicious software and recognise unsafe websites.

3. **Identity Theft**: Through compromised data, hackers can steal personal information and use it for fraudulent purposes, such as opening credit accounts or making unauthorised purchases.

4. **Cyberbullying**: A persistent issue in digital environments, cyberbullying involves harassment, threats, or insults directed at individuals through online platforms. Understanding how to prevent, report, and respond to cyberbullying is a key element of online safety.

5. **Online Predators**: Some individuals use the internet to exploit young users, building trust with the intent of harm. Educators must raise awareness about the tactics used by predators and how students can protect themselves.

6. **Inappropriate Content**: Exposure to harmful or inappropriate content, such as violence, hate speech, or explicit material, is an unfortunate reality of the online world. Filtering tools and digital literacy can help students navigate away from such content.

Building a Culture of Cyber Safety in Schools

Establishing a culture of cyber safety involves both proactive teaching and creating a secure digital environment within schools. Educators play a crucial role in equipping students with the knowledge and skills to stay safe online, and it's important to ensure that schools model good cyber hygiene practices.

1. The Role of Cyber Hygiene in Online Safety

Cyber hygiene refers to a set of habits that ensure online safety and security. Just as personal hygiene prevents illness, cyber hygiene helps prevent cyber threats. Key practices include:

- **Strong Password Practices**: Students should be taught to create complex, unique passwords for each account and to avoid sharing them with others. Password management tools can be introduced as a way to store passwords securely.

- **Two-Factor Authentication (2FA)**: This extra layer of security involves a second form of verification (such as a text message code) beyond a password. Educators should encourage students to enable 2FA on their accounts to enhance security.

- **Regular Software Updates**: Updates often contain patches for security vulnerabilities, so students must be taught the importance of keeping their software and devices up-to-date.

- **Safe Browsing Habits**: Students should understand how to identify secure websites (those with "https" and a padlock symbol) and avoid entering personal information on unverified sites.

2. Teaching Students About Privacy Settings

Students often share personal details online without considering the long-term implications. Educators can help by demonstrating how to adjust **privacy settings** on social media, messaging platforms, and other digital services. Lessons should include:

- **Limiting Data Sharing**: Encourage students to think carefully before sharing personal information such as home addresses, phone numbers, or their location online.

- **Understanding Terms and Conditions**: Few students (or adults) take the time to read the fine print before agreeing to it. Educators should raise awareness about what data they may be agreeing to share with third-party services.

- **Managing Social Media Profiles**: Students need to know how to control who can view their profiles, posts, and personal information on platforms like Instagram, TikTok, and Facebook.

3. Encouraging Responsible Digital Citizenship

Digital citizenship involves using technology responsibly and ethically. A responsible digital citizen not only protects their own privacy and security but also respects others online. Educators can promote responsible behaviour by:

- **Setting Guidelines for Online Communication**: Establish clear rules for respectful communication in online spaces, including class forums, social media, and messaging apps.

- **Avoiding Oversharing**: Students should be mindful of the information they share online. Even seemingly harmless details can be exploited by malicious actors.

- **Reporting Unsafe or Suspicious Behaviour**: Encourage students to report any inappropriate behaviour, threats, or bullying they experience or witness online.

Cyber Safety Tools and Resources for Educators

To support cyber safety education, numerous tools and resources are available for educators. Incorporating these into lessons can enhance learning and help students put theory into practice.

1. **Digital Safety Workshops**: Interactive workshops on cyber safety can make abstract concepts more tangible. Topics could include password management, recognising phishing scams, and safe online communication.

2. **Cyber Safety Games and Simulations**: Gamified tools allow students to learn cyber safety in an engaging way. For instance, platforms like **"Interland"** (by Google) teach children about phishing, password safety, and data protection through interactive games.

3. **Parental Involvement**: Educators should encourage parents to take an active role in their children's cyber safety education. This can include offering resources or holding workshops for parents on topics like privacy settings, filtering tools, and monitoring online activity.

Creating Safe Spaces for Open Discussions

An important aspect of teaching cyber safety is creating an environment where students feel comfortable discussing their concerns about the internet and social media. Open discussions can provide insights into how students are interacting online and offer opportunities to address any safety gaps.

1. **Cyber Safety Conversations**: Regular conversations in classrooms about current online safety trends and risks can keep students engaged and informed.

2. **Anonymous Reporting Systems**: Schools should offer students a way to anonymously report incidents of cyberbullying, harassment, or unsafe online behaviour. This encourages students to speak out without fear of repercussions.

3. **Peer Mentoring**: Schools can establish peer mentoring systems where older students teach younger students about online safety. This peer-to-peer learning approach can be highly effective and relatable for students.

The Role of Legislation and School Policies

While educators play a hands-on role in teaching cyber safety, broader legal frameworks and school policies are crucial for creating a safer digital environment. Schools should ensure that their policies are up-to-date with relevant legislation and reflect the realities of the digital world.

- **Data Protection Laws**: Students should be introduced to important legal frameworks such as the **General Data Protection Regulation (GDPR)**, which governs how personal data is collected, stored, and used. Understanding these laws empowers students to take control of their digital identities.

- **School Internet Policies**: Schools must have clear policies regarding the use of school networks and devices, including acceptable use policies (AUPs). Students should understand the consequences of violating these policies and the importance of respecting digital boundaries.

Case Studies in Cyber Safety Education

1. **Cyber Safety Workshops in Secondary Schools**: Several UK secondary schools have introduced comprehensive cyber safety workshops that teach students how to recognise phishing scams and manage privacy settings on social media. These workshops often involve real-world examples and interactive activities, making the concepts easier to grasp.

2. **University Data Security Programs**: Universities have implemented data security programs that focus on protecting student information. By teaching students about encryption, secure passwords, and responsible data sharing, these programs help foster a culture of cyber awareness on campus.

Conclusion

Educators play a pivotal role in equipping students with the skills to navigate the digital world securely. Through teaching cyber hygiene, responsible online behaviour, and privacy awareness, educators can empower students to protect themselves from cyber threats and contribute to safer online communities.

The next chapter will explore how educators can teach **digital literacy**—helping students critically evaluate the vast amount of information they encounter online and make informed, responsible decisions in a complex digital landscape.

Chapter 8: Integrating Digital Literacy into the Curriculum

The Importance of Digital Literacy in Education

In an era where information is abundant and constantly evolving, the ability to critically assess and interact with digital content is paramount. **Digital literacy** encompasses a range of skills, including the ability to find, evaluate, create, and communicate information using digital platforms. As educators, it is essential to equip students with these skills to navigate the complex online world responsibly and effectively. This chapter explores the integration of digital literacy into the educational curriculum, providing strategies and best practices for educators.

Defining Digital Literacy

Digital literacy goes beyond mere technical skills or knowing how to use devices. It involves:

1. **Finding Information**: The ability to effectively search for relevant content using various digital tools and search engines.

2. **Evaluating Information**: Critical thinking skills to assess the credibility, bias, and accuracy of online content.

3. **Creating Content**: The skills to produce digital media, including writing, video production, and design, while adhering to ethical standards.

4. **Communicating Responsibly**: Understanding how to communicate effectively in digital spaces, including respecting others and maintaining online etiquette.

5. **Understanding Digital Rights and Responsibilities**: Awareness of legal and ethical issues related to online behaviour, including copyright laws, privacy rights, and responsible digital citizenship.

The Role of Digital Literacy in 21st-Century Skills

Digital literacy is a critical component of the **21st-century skills framework**, which emphasises collaboration, communication, creativity, and critical thinking. Students need to be proficient in digital literacy to succeed academically and professionally in a rapidly changing landscape.

- **Collaboration**: Digital tools facilitate collaboration among students, enabling them to work together on projects in real time. Educators should teach students how to use collaborative platforms effectively while respecting each other's contributions.

- **Creativity**: Digital literacy encourages creativity, as students learn to express themselves through various media. Teaching them how to use digital tools for content creation empowers them to become producers, not just consumers, of information.

- **Critical Thinking**: As students engage with diverse online content, they must develop critical thinking skills to analyse and synthesise information. Educators should create assignments that challenge students to question the validity of sources and draw connections between different ideas.

Strategies for Integrating Digital Literacy into the Curriculum

1. **Curriculum Mapping for Digital Literacy**: Schools can incorporate digital literacy across subjects by mapping out where these skills fit within existing curricula. Educators should identify opportunities to integrate digital literacy into lessons, whether in language arts, social studies, science, or mathematics.

2. **Project-Based Learning**: Engaging students in project-based learning (PBL) provides real-world contexts for applying digital literacy skills. Students can undertake projects that require them to research topics, evaluate sources, create presentations, and collaborate with peers. PBL promotes active learning and critical thinking.

3. **Digital Literacy Modules**: Schools can develop standalone digital literacy modules as part of the curriculum. These modules can cover topics such as

information evaluation, ethical online behaviour, and content creation. They can be delivered through workshops, online courses, or integrated into existing classes.

4. **Collaboration with Media and Information Specialists**: Partnering with librarians and media specialists can enhance digital literacy education. These professionals can offer expertise in information retrieval and evaluation, guiding students through research processes and resource utilisation.

5. **Incorporating Technology in Classrooms**: Providing students access to technology, such as computers, tablets, and digital tools, is crucial for developing digital literacy skills. Educators should leverage technology for both instruction and student learning, ensuring that students are comfortable using various tools.

Teaching Students to Evaluate Digital Content

An essential aspect of digital literacy is teaching students how to evaluate the credibility and reliability of information. The following strategies can help:

1. **The CRAAP Test**: Introduce the CRAAP Test (Currency, Relevance, Authority, Accuracy, Purpose) as a framework for evaluating sources. Students can use this checklist to assess the quality of information they encounter online.

- Currency: Is the information up-to-date?

- Relevance: Does it address the research question or topic?

- Authority: Who is the author or publisher? Are they reputable?

- Accuracy: Is the information supported by evidence? Are there citations?

- Purpose: What is the intent of the information? Is it biased?

2. **Source Comparison Exercises**: Encourage students to compare multiple sources on the same topic. This exercise helps them recognise different perspectives and understand how bias can influence information.

3. **Fact-Checking Resources**: Familiarise students with reliable fact-checking websites (such as Snopes, FactCheck.org, or PolitiFact). Teaching them how to verify claims enhances their ability to discern fact from fiction.

Fostering Responsible Content Creation

As students learn to create their digital content, it's essential to teach them about ethical considerations and responsible practices:

1. **Copyright and Fair Use**: Educate students about copyright laws, fair use, and the importance of respecting intellectual property. Encourage them to seek permission for using others' work and to give proper credit through citations.

2. **Digital Footprint Awareness**: Help students understand that their online actions contribute to their digital footprint. They should be mindful of what they post, as it can affect their reputation and future opportunities.

3. **Encouraging Positive Contributions**: Teach students the value of contributing positively to online communities. This can include sharing constructive feedback, promoting kindness, and standing against misinformation.

Assessment of Digital Literacy Skills

Evaluating students' digital literacy skills is essential to ensure they are mastering these competencies. Consider the following assessment methods:

1. **Rubrics for Digital Projects**: Create rubrics that outline criteria for evaluating students' digital projects. Assessments can include the effectiveness of research, the quality of content creation, and adherence to ethical standards.

2. **Reflective Journals**: Encourage students to maintain reflective journals documenting their experiences with digital literacy skills. This helps them articulate their learning and identify areas for improvement.

3. **Peer Assessment**: Incorporate peer assessment to foster collaboration and accountability. Students can provide feedback to each other on digital projects, fostering a sense of community and shared learning.

Conclusion

Integrating digital literacy into the curriculum is essential for preparing students to navigate the complexities of the digital age. By providing students with the skills to find, evaluate, create, and communicate information responsibly, educators empower them to become informed digital citizens.

In the next chapter, we will explore **social media etiquette in the classroom**, emphasising the importance of respectful and responsible online behaviour in academic settings. This chapter will provide practical strategies for teaching students how to engage positively in digital communication and avoid common pitfalls.

Chapter 9: Navigating Social Media in Education

The Ubiquity of Social Media in Students' Lives

Social media has become an integral part of students' daily lives, influencing their communication patterns, social interactions, and even their learning experiences. With platforms like Facebook, Instagram, TikTok, Snapchat, and Twitter dominating the digital landscape, it is crucial for educators to understand how these platforms affect students and how to integrate them positively into educational settings.

The Positive Aspects of Social Media

1. **Enhanced Communication and Collaboration**: Social media offers tools that facilitate communication and collaboration among students and educators. Platforms like Google Classroom, Edmodo, and Microsoft Teams create spaces for students to engage in discussions, share resources, and collaborate on projects.

2. **Access to Resources and Information**: Social media provides students with access to a wealth of information and educational resources. Educators can direct students to follow relevant pages, groups, or hashtags that can enhance their learning experience.

3. **Building Community and Support**: Social media allows students to connect with peers who share similar interests, fostering a sense of community. This is particularly valuable for students in remote or underserved areas, as they can engage with a global audience.

4. **Opportunities for Self-Expression**: Students can use social media as a platform for self-expression, creativity, and advocacy. Encouraging them to share their thoughts and ideas can help develop their voices and promote civic engagement.

Understanding the Challenges of Social Media in Education

Despite the potential benefits, social media poses challenges that educators must address:

1. **Distraction and Procrastination**: The allure of social media can be a significant distraction for students. Educators should acknowledge this reality and create strategies to minimise distractions while maximising engagement.

2. **Cyberbullying and Toxic Behaviour**: Social media can amplify negative behaviours, such as cyberbullying and harassment. Educators need to establish clear guidelines on acceptable behaviour and provide resources for students to report and address such incidents.

3. **Privacy Concerns**: Students often share personal information on social media, sometimes without understanding the implications. Educators should teach students about privacy settings, the importance of safeguarding personal information, and the potential risks of oversharing.

4. **Misinformation and Manipulation**: The spread of misinformation on social media can impact students' understanding of important issues. Educators must teach students how to discern credible sources from unreliable ones and to approach information critically.

Teaching Social Media Etiquette in the Classroom

To ensure students engage responsibly on social media, educators can implement the following strategies:

1. **Establishing Guidelines**: Create a set of guidelines for appropriate online behaviour in educational contexts. These guidelines should cover aspects such as respect for others, constructive criticism, and the importance of maintaining professionalism.

2. **Encouraging Empathy and Respect**: Teach students the significance of empathy in their online interactions. Emphasise that tone can be easily misunderstood in written communication and encourage them to consider the feelings of others when posting comments or sharing content.

3. **Role-Playing Scenarios**: Engage students in role-playing scenarios where they navigate social media situations, such as responding to negative comments or dealing with cyberbullying. This hands-on approach allows students to practise appropriate responses in a safe environment.

4. **Promoting Positive Content Creation**: Encourage students to create and share positive, constructive content. Assign projects that involve developing campaigns or initiatives that promote kindness, awareness, or social causes.

Integrating Social Media into Educational Practice

Educators can leverage social media as a teaching tool in various ways:

1. **Classroom Discussions**: Use social media platforms to facilitate classroom discussions. For instance, educators can create private Facebook groups or Twitter hashtags for students to share insights, ask questions, and engage in discussions related to course content.

2. **Curating Resources**: Encourage students to curate content related to their studies by following educational accounts, engaging with thought leaders, and participating in relevant discussions. This helps them stay informed and connected to their fields of interest.

3. **Flipped Classrooms**: Implement a flipped classroom model by using social media to share instructional materials and resources. Students can review content before class, allowing for more interactive and collaborative in-class activities.

4. **Showcasing Student Work**: Utilize social media to showcase students' achievements and projects. Highlighting their work on school social media accounts can foster a sense of pride and community while also promoting positive school culture.

Addressing Privacy and Safety Concerns

When incorporating social media into education, educators must prioritise student privacy and safety:

1. **Educating on Privacy Settings**: Teach students how to adjust privacy settings on their social media accounts. Ensure they understand the importance of keeping personal information private and only sharing content with trusted individuals.

2. **Promoting Responsible Sharing**: Discuss the potential consequences of sharing personal information or sensitive content online. Encourage students to think critically about what they post and who can see it.

3. **Creating a Reporting System**: Establish a clear process for reporting inappropriate behaviour or content. Ensure students know they can speak to trusted adults if they encounter harassment or bullying online.

Conclusion

As social media continues to play a prominent role in students' lives, educators must find ways to integrate it positively into the classroom while addressing its challenges. By teaching social media etiquette, promoting responsible behaviour, and leveraging its potential as a learning tool, educators can help students navigate the digital landscape effectively.

In the next chapter, we will explore **the importance of privacy and security in the digital age**, emphasising how educators can equip students with the knowledge and skills needed to protect their personal information and navigate online threats.

Chapter 10: Privacy and Security in the Digital Age

Understanding Privacy in the Digital Landscape

In today's interconnected world, privacy has become a paramount concern for individuals, especially for students who are often less aware of the implications of sharing personal information online. Educators play a critical role in guiding students through the complexities of digital privacy, ensuring they understand how to protect their information and navigate the online environment safely.

The Importance of Digital Privacy

1. **Personal Data Protection**: With increasing amounts of personal data being shared on social media and other digital platforms, understanding privacy settings and data protection laws is crucial. Students need to grasp how their personal information can be collected, stored, and potentially misused by third parties.

2. **Empowerment Through Knowledge**: By teaching students about privacy, educators empower them to take control of their digital lives. When students understand their rights and the implications of their online actions, they can make informed decisions about what to share and with whom.

3. **Impact of Digital Footprint**: Students should be made aware of the concept of a digital footprint—the trail of data they leave behind through their online activities. Educators can explain how this digital footprint can impact their future opportunities, including college admissions and employment prospects.

Data Protection Basics for Students

1. **Understanding Privacy Settings**: Educators must emphasise the importance of reviewing and adjusting privacy settings on social media platforms. Students should learn how to limit who can see their posts, who can contact them, and how to manage their friend or follower lists.

2. **Personal Information to Avoid Sharing**: Students should be educated about the types of information that are sensitive and should not be shared online, such as home addresses, phone numbers, and financial details.

3. **Recognising Public vs. Private Spaces**: It's important for students to understand the difference between public and private spaces online. Educators can explain how information shared in public forums can be accessed by anyone, whereas information shared in private groups or direct messages is more secure.

Understanding Cyber Threats

In addition to privacy concerns, students must be aware of various cyber threats they might encounter:

1. **Phishing Attacks**: Educators should teach students how to recognise phishing attempts—fraudulent messages that appear to be from legitimate sources but are designed to steal personal information. This includes identifying suspicious emails, texts, and links.

2. **Malware and Viruses**: Understanding malware and viruses is essential. Students should learn about the importance of antivirus software and safe browsing practices, such as avoiding downloads from untrusted sources.

3. **Online Predators**: Educators should provide information about online predators and the tactics they use to manipulate young users. Teaching students to be cautious about sharing personal information with strangers online is vital.

Creating a Culture of Safety in Schools

1. **Establishing Clear Policies**: Schools should develop clear policies regarding online behaviour and privacy. These policies should outline acceptable online conduct and the consequences of violating them.

2. **Providing Resources for Support**: Schools should offer resources for students to seek help if they feel uncomfortable or unsafe online. This includes having trusted adults, like teachers or counsellors, available for guidance.

3. **Encouraging Open Discussions**: Foster an environment where students feel comfortable discussing their online experiences, including any concerns they may have about privacy or security. Open dialogues can help address fears and misconceptions.

Teaching Students to Safeguard Personal Data

1. **Promoting Strong Password Practices**: Educators should instruct students on the importance of creating strong, unique passwords for their accounts. Teaching them to use password managers can help them maintain security across various platforms.

2. **Encouraging Regular Monitoring**: Encourage students to regularly monitor their online accounts for any suspicious activity. Teaching them to review their privacy settings periodically ensures that they stay informed about who can access their information.

3. **Instilling a Critical Mindset**: Equip students with the skills to think critically about the information they encounter online. This includes questioning the credibility of sources, recognising advertisements disguised as genuine content, and understanding the motives behind certain information.

Conclusion

As students navigate the complexities of the digital age, educators must equip them with the tools and knowledge necessary to protect their privacy and security online. By fostering an understanding of digital privacy, teaching about cyber threats, and creating a culture of safety in schools, educators can empower students to engage in the digital world responsibly and confidently.

In the next chapter, we will explore **the role of critical thinking in digital literacy**, discussing how educators can help students develop the analytical skills needed to navigate the vast amounts of information available online.

Chapter 11: Critical Thinking in the Digital Age

Understanding the Importance of Critical Thinking

In an era where information is abundant and easily accessible, fostering critical thinking skills in students is more important than ever. Critical thinking enables individuals to analyse, evaluate, and synthesise information, allowing them to make informed decisions and navigate the complexities of the digital landscape effectively. This chapter focuses on the role of critical thinking in digital literacy, exploring how educators can cultivate these essential skills in their students.

Defining Critical Thinking

1. **What is Critical Thinking?**: Critical thinking is the ability to think clearly and rationally, understanding the logical connection between ideas. It involves questioning assumptions, evaluating evidence, and making reasoned conclusions based on analysis rather than emotion.

2. **The Role of Critical Thinking in Digital Literacy**: In the context of digital literacy, critical thinking allows students to discern credible sources from misinformation, recognise biases in content, and understand the motives behind the information they consume.

The Impact of Misinformation and Fake News

1. **The Proliferation of Misinformation**: The rise of social media and digital platforms has led to the rapid spread of misinformation and fake news. Educators must prepare students to identify and challenge false narratives, which can have serious consequences for individuals and society.

2. **Recognising Cognitive Bias**: Students should be educated about cognitive biases that affect their judgment, such as confirmation bias, where individuals favour information that confirms their pre-existing beliefs.

Recognising these biases is essential for fostering objective analysis of information.

Teaching Critical Thinking Skills

1. **Encouraging Questioning**: Educators should create an environment that encourages students to ask questions and seek deeper understanding. This can involve prompting students to consider the "who, what, where, when, and why" of the information they encounter.

2. **Evaluating Sources**: Teach students to assess the credibility of sources by examining the author's credentials, the publication's reputation, and the quality of the evidence presented. Providing checklists for evaluating sources can be a practical tool in the classroom.

3. **Analysis of Media Messages**: Engage students in activities that require them to analyse media messages, such as advertisements, news articles, and social media posts. This can help students understand how media can be crafted to persuade or manipulate.

4. **Debate and Discussion**: Incorporating structured debates and discussions in the classroom encourages students to articulate their thoughts, consider opposing viewpoints, and back up their arguments with evidence. This practice enhances their ability to think critically and engage with diverse perspectives.

5. **Problem-Solving Activities**: Use real-world scenarios and case studies to help students apply critical thinking to solve problems. This approach encourages them to analyse information, weigh options, and develop reasoned solutions.

Integrating Critical Thinking Across the Curriculum

1. **Cross-Disciplinary Approaches**: Critical thinking should not be confined to a single subject area. Educators can integrate critical thinking skills into various subjects, encouraging students to apply these skills in different contexts.

2. **Project-Based Learning**: Implement project-based learning initiatives that require students to research, analyse, and present their findings on a specific topic. This approach fosters collaboration and deepens understanding.

3. **Reflective Practices**: Encourage students to engage in reflective practices, such as journaling or self-assessment, to evaluate their own thought processes and decision-making. This can help them become more aware of their critical thinking skills.

Fostering a Culture of Critical Thinking

1. **Creating a Safe Space for Exploration**: Establish a classroom environment where students feel comfortable expressing their thoughts and

challenging ideas. This encourages open dialogue and a willingness to engage with complex topics.

2. **Role of Educators as Facilitators**: Educators should position themselves as facilitators of learning, guiding students in their exploration of critical thinking rather than simply imparting information. This approach encourages independence and self-directed learning.

3. **Assessment of Critical Thinking**: Develop assessment methods that evaluate students' critical thinking skills, such as reflective essays, presentations, or portfolios. This encourages students to take their critical thinking seriously and strive for improvement.

Conclusion

Critical thinking is an indispensable skill for navigating the digital landscape. By equipping students with the tools to analyse information critically, educators can help them become informed citizens capable of engaging thoughtfully with the world around them. As we move to the next chapter, we will explore **how to address the challenges of social media in educational settings**, focusing on strategies to promote healthy online interactions among students.

Chapter 12: Addressing the Challenges of Social Media in Educational Settings

Understanding the Social Media Landscape

Social media has become an integral part of students' lives, shaping their

interactions, identity formation, and communication styles. While these platforms

offer opportunities for connection and learning, they also present numerous challenges that educators must address. This chapter explores the complexities of social media in educational settings and provides strategies for fostering a positive digital environment.

The Influence of Social Media on Student Behaviour

1. **Social Dynamics**: Social media influences how students interact with peers, form relationships, and navigate social hierarchies. Educators need to understand the dynamics of these interactions, including the impact of likes, comments, and followers on self-esteem and social validation.

2. **Digital Identity and Self-Representation**: Social media platforms allow students to curate their identities, which can lead to both positive and negative outcomes. The pressure to maintain a certain image can affect mental health and well-being, necessitating discussions around authenticity and self-acceptance.

3. **Peer Pressure and Comparison**: The pervasive nature of social media can create a culture of comparison, where students feel pressured to meet unrealistic standards set by their peers. This phenomenon can lead to anxiety, depression, and a distorted sense of self-worth.

Challenges of Social Media in Education

1. **Distraction and Engagement**: While social media can be a valuable educational tool, it can also serve as a significant distraction during class.

Educators must balance the benefits of social media with the need for focused learning.

2. **Cyberbullying and Toxic Behaviour**: The anonymity provided by social media can encourage negative behaviour, such as cyberbullying, trolling, and harassment. Educators must implement strategies to prevent and address these issues effectively.

3. **Misinformation and Fake News**: The rapid spread of misinformation on social media can lead to confusion and misinformed beliefs among students. Teaching students to critically evaluate information sources is essential for combating this challenge.

Strategies for Managing Social Media in the Classroom

1. **Establishing Clear Guidelines**: Develop clear policies regarding the use of social media in educational settings. These guidelines should outline acceptable behaviour, consequences for violations, and the expected use of social media for learning purposes.

2. **Incorporating Social Media in Learning**: Leverage social media as a teaching tool by integrating it into the curriculum. For example, educators can use platforms like Twitter for discussions, create class blogs, or encourage students to share research on relevant platforms.

3. **Promoting Digital Citizenship**: Educate students about digital citizenship, emphasising responsible and respectful online behaviour. This education should include discussions about privacy, online safety, and the impact of their actions on others.

4. **Fostering Open Communication**: Encourage students to communicate openly about their social media experiences. Creating a safe space for discussions can help students feel supported and understood, allowing them to share their challenges and successes.

5. **Teaching Conflict Resolution**: Equip students with the skills to navigate conflicts that may arise on social media. Teaching them how to address disagreements respectfully and constructively is crucial for fostering positive interactions.

6. **Utilising Technology to Monitor Usage**: Implement tools that help monitor students' social media usage in a respectful and ethical manner. These tools can provide insights into students' online behaviour, helping educators address potential issues proactively.

Creating a Positive Social Media Culture

1. **Celebrating Positive Online Behaviour**: Recognise and celebrate instances of positive online interactions among students. This can be done through awards, shout-outs in class, or showcasing student achievements on school social media channels.

2. **Encouraging Peer Support**: Foster a culture of peer support where students help one another navigate social media challenges. Implementing mentorship programmes or peer-led workshops can facilitate this process.

3. **Parental Involvement**: Engage parents in discussions about social media and its impact on their children. Providing resources and guidance for parents can empower them to support their children's responsible use of social media at home.

4. **Continual Professional Development for Educators**: Educators should engage in ongoing professional development focused on social media trends and best practices for managing social media in educational settings. Staying informed allows educators to address challenges more effectively.

Conclusion

While social media poses challenges in educational settings, it also offers opportunities for engagement and connection. By addressing the complexities of social media, educators can create a balanced approach that maximises its benefits while minimising its drawbacks. In the next chapter, we will explore **the intersection of social media and mental health**, discussing how educators can support students' well-being in the digital age.

Chapter 13: The Intersection of Social Media and Mental Health

Understanding the Impact of Social Media on Mental Health

In recent years, significant attention has been directed towards the impact of social media on mental health, particularly among students. While social media platforms can provide valuable opportunities for connection and self-expression, they also have the potential to contribute to mental health challenges. This chapter delves into the nuanced relationship between social media use and mental health, providing educators with insights and strategies to support student well-being.

Positive Aspects of Social Media

1. **Community and Support**: Social media can foster a sense of community and belonging, allowing students to connect with peers who share similar interests, experiences, or challenges. Online support groups can offer encouragement and validation, particularly for those dealing with mental health issues.

2. **Access to Resources**: Many mental health organisations use social media to disseminate information, resources, and coping strategies. Educators can encourage students to seek out reputable sources and engage with content that promotes mental well-being.

3. **Self-Expression and Creativity**: Platforms like Instagram and TikTok provide avenues for self-expression and creativity, allowing students to share their thoughts, art, and experiences. Engaging in creative activities can serve as a form of therapy and boost self-esteem.

Negative Aspects of Social Media

1. **Comparison and Self-Esteem Issues**: The constant exposure to curated images and idealised representations of life can lead students to compare

themselves unfavourably to others. This phenomenon can result in feelings of inadequacy, anxiety, and depression.

2. **Cyberbullying and Harassment**: As previously discussed, social media can be a breeding ground for cyberbullying and toxic behaviour. Victims of cyberbullying often experience heightened anxiety, depression, and isolation.

3. **Fear of Missing Out (FOMO)**: The pervasive nature of social media can create a sense of FOMO, where students feel anxious about not participating in social events or experiences shared online. This anxiety can lead to social withdrawal and increased feelings of loneliness.

4. **Addiction and Compulsive Use**: Excessive social media use can lead to addictive behaviours, impacting students' ability to focus on academic tasks and engage in face-to-face interactions. This addiction can exacerbate feelings of isolation and contribute to mental health decline.

Recognising Signs of Mental Health Issues

Educators play a crucial role in identifying students who may be struggling with mental health issues exacerbated by social media. Some signs to watch for include:

- Changes in behaviour, such as withdrawal from social activities or a decline in academic performance.

- Increased absenteeism from school or reluctance to participate in group activities.

- Expressions of distress or anxiety related to social media interactions.

- Physical signs of stress, such as changes in appetite or sleep patterns.

Strategies for Supporting Student Mental Health

1. **Creating a Safe and Supportive Environment**: Establish a classroom culture that promotes open dialogue about mental health. Encourage students to share their experiences and seek help when needed.

2. **Integrating Mental Health Education**: Include mental health education in the curriculum, emphasising the importance of well-being and resilience. This education should address the impact of social media and provide strategies for managing online interactions.

3. **Encouraging Healthy Social Media Use**: Teach students about balanced social media usage, including setting boundaries and taking regular breaks. Encourage mindfulness practices to help students manage their online presence.

4. **Promoting Critical Thinking**: Equip students with critical thinking skills to evaluate the content they encounter on social media. Encourage them to question the authenticity of the information and images they see and to recognise the potential impact on their mental health.

5. **Providing Resources**: Share mental health resources, hotlines, and support groups with students. Make sure they know where to turn for help and how to access support.

6. **Collaboration with Mental Health Professionals**: Work closely with school counsellors and mental health professionals to identify students in need and create intervention strategies. Professional guidance can enhance educators' ability to address mental health issues effectively.

Fostering Resilience in Students

1. **Developing Coping Strategies**: Teach students coping strategies to manage stress and anxiety, such as mindfulness exercises, journaling, and engaging in physical activity.

2. **Encouraging Positive Relationships**: Promote the importance of building healthy relationships both online and offline. Foster peer support networks that encourage empathy and understanding.

3. **Celebrating Achievements**: Acknowledge and celebrate students' achievements, both big and small, to boost self-esteem and create a sense of accomplishment.

4. **Involving Parents and Guardians**: Engage parents in discussions about the impact of social media on mental health. Provide them with resources to support their children's well-being at home.

Conclusion

Understanding the intersection of social media and mental health is crucial for educators navigating the complexities of the digital landscape. By fostering a supportive environment and equipping students with the tools to manage their online experiences, educators can play a pivotal role in promoting mental well-being. In the next chapter, we will explore **the role of parental involvement in supporting students' digital literacy and mental health**, discussing how families can work together with schools to create a holistic approach to education in the digital age.

Chapter 14: The Role of Parental Involvement in Digital Literacy and Mental Health

Understanding the Importance of Parental Engagement

In the digital age, parental involvement plays a crucial role in shaping children's experiences with technology and social media. Educators must recognise the significance of collaborating with parents to create a supportive environment for students, both academically and emotionally. This chapter explores the various ways parents can be involved in their children's digital literacy and mental health, providing educators with strategies to foster this collaboration.

The Impact of Parental Involvement

1. **Enhanced Learning Outcomes**: Research consistently shows that active parental involvement in a child's education leads to improved academic performance. When parents engage in discussions about digital literacy, students are more likely to develop critical thinking skills and responsible online behaviour.

2. **Open Communication**: When parents are involved, students feel more comfortable discussing their online experiences, including challenges and successes. This open dialogue can help identify potential issues early and create opportunities for guidance and support.

3. **Modelling Healthy Behaviours**: Parents serve as role models for their children. By demonstrating healthy technology usage and communication practices, parents can instil similar habits in their children, promoting digital etiquette and responsible online behaviour.

4. **Emotional Support**: Parents who are informed about their children's online activities can provide the necessary emotional support when challenges arise. This support can be vital for addressing issues related to cyberbullying, social media anxiety, and the pressures of online interactions.

Strategies for Engaging Parents in Digital Literacy

1. **Workshops and Information Sessions**: Organise workshops and informational sessions for parents that focus on digital literacy, social media etiquette, and the mental health implications of technology use. Providing practical advice and resources can empower parents to better support their children.

2. **Regular Communication**: Maintain consistent communication with parents about their children's progress and challenges in the digital realm. Use newsletters, emails, or dedicated platforms to share resources and tips for fostering digital literacy at home.

3. **Encourage Participation in School Activities**: Invite parents to participate in school activities that focus on digital literacy and mental health. This could include guest speaker events, panel discussions, or collaborative projects that encourage parental involvement.

4. **Create Parent-Child Learning Activities**: Encourage parents to engage in learning activities with their children that promote digital literacy. For example, parents and children can work together to evaluate online content, engage in coding exercises, or explore the implications of digital footprints.

5. **Share Online Resources**: Provide parents with a curated list of online resources that focus on digital literacy and mental health. This may include

articles, videos, and guides that help parents understand the complexities of the digital landscape.

Empowering Parents to Address Mental Health

1. **Identifying Signs of Distress**: Educate parents on the signs of mental health challenges in children, such as changes in mood, behaviour, or social interactions. This knowledge enables parents to be proactive in seeking help for their children.

2. **Promoting Healthy Technology Habits**: Offer strategies for parents to encourage healthy technology use at home. This may include setting screen time limits, fostering offline activities, and encouraging breaks from social media.

3. **Facilitating Discussions on Online Experiences**: Encourage parents to initiate conversations about their children's online experiences, including social media interactions, gaming, and digital friendships. These discussions can help children feel supported and understood.

4. **Building Emotional Resilience**: Teach parents techniques for fostering emotional resilience in their children. This may include mindfulness practices, coping strategies for managing stress, and promoting a growth mindset.

5. **Encouraging Professional Help When Needed**: Provide parents with resources to identify and access mental health support services for their children. This may include local mental health professionals, hotlines, and online support groups.

Fostering a Collaborative Relationship Between Parents and Educators

1. **Parent-Teacher Conferences**: Use parent-teacher conferences as an opportunity to discuss digital literacy and mental health. Share observations about students' online behaviour and collaborate with parents to develop strategies for support.

2. **Involvement in Curriculum Development**: Encourage parents to participate in discussions about curriculum development related to digital literacy and mental health education. Their insights can enhance the relevance and effectiveness of educational programmes.

3. **Feedback Mechanisms**: Establish feedback mechanisms that allow parents to share their perspectives on digital literacy initiatives and mental health resources. This input can help educators refine their approaches and better address the needs of students and families.

4. **Community Partnerships**: Build partnerships with local organisations that focus on digital literacy and mental health. Collaborating with these organisations can provide additional resources and support for parents and educators.

Conclusion

Parental involvement is a critical component of supporting students in navigating the digital landscape. By fostering collaboration between parents and educators, we can create a holistic approach to digital literacy and mental health that benefits students' overall well-being. In the next chapter, we will explore **the future of education in the digital age**, discussing emerging trends, challenges, and opportunities for educators in preparing students for success in an increasingly digital world.

Chapter 15: The Future of Education in the Digital Age

Emerging Trends in Digital Education

The landscape of education is undergoing a transformative shift due to the rapid advancement of technology and the pervasive influence of the internet and social media. As educators look toward the future, it is crucial to identify emerging trends that will shape the way we teach and learn. This chapter explores several key trends that are likely to define the future of education in the digital age.

1. Personalised Learning

Personalised learning is an educational approach that tailors instruction to meet the individual needs, interests, and abilities of each student. With the help of technology, educators can leverage data and analytics to create personalised learning experiences. This trend is characterised by:

- **Adaptive Learning Technologies**: Platforms that adjust the difficulty of tasks based on student performance, allowing for a customised learning journey.

- **Student-Centred Approaches**: Encouraging students to take an active role in their learning by selecting topics, projects, and pacing that align with their interests and strengths.

- **Real-Time Feedback**: Providing immediate feedback through digital assessments, enabling students to reflect on their progress and make adjustments as needed.

2. Blended Learning Environments

Blended learning combines traditional face-to-face instruction with online learning, creating a more flexible and engaging educational experience. This model offers several benefits, including:

- **Flexibility**: Students can access resources and complete assignments at their own pace and convenience.

- **Increased Engagement**: Interactive online content and collaborative projects foster greater student engagement and participation.

- **Access to Diverse Resources**: Educators can incorporate a variety of digital tools, multimedia resources, and global perspectives into their teaching.

3. Gamification of Education

Gamification involves integrating game elements into educational experiences to enhance motivation and engagement. This trend is gaining traction in classrooms, with features such as:

- **Point Systems and Badges**: Rewarding students for achieving learning milestones and completing tasks, creating a sense of accomplishment.

- **Interactive Learning Environments**: Using game-based platforms to teach complex concepts in a fun and immersive manner.

- **Collaborative Challenges**: Encouraging teamwork and collaboration through group challenges and competitions.

4. Social and Emotional Learning (SEL)

As awareness of the importance of mental health and emotional well-being grows, educators are increasingly incorporating Social and Emotional Learning (SEL) into curricula. SEL focuses on developing essential life skills, including:

- **Self-Awareness**: Helping students recognise their emotions, strengths, and areas for growth.

- **Relationship Skills**: Teaching effective communication, empathy, and conflict resolution strategies.

- **Responsible Decision-Making**: Encouraging students to consider the consequences of their actions and make informed choices.

5. Digital Citizenship Education

As digital interactions become integral to daily life, educating students on responsible online behaviour is paramount. Digital citizenship education encompasses:

- **Understanding Online Etiquette**: Teaching students how to communicate respectfully and responsibly in digital environments.

- **Awareness of Privacy and Security**: Empowering students to protect their personal information and navigate online risks.

- **Critical Media Literacy**: Equipping students with the skills to evaluate the credibility of online content and recognise misinformation.

Challenges Facing Educators

While the future of education is promising, educators must navigate several challenges to effectively implement these trends:

- **Equity and Access**: Ensuring all students have access to technology and resources is crucial for personalised learning and digital citizenship education.

- **Professional Development**: Educators need ongoing training and support to integrate new technologies and pedagogies into their teaching practices.

- **Balancing Screen Time**: Finding the right balance between digital and face-to-face interactions is essential for fostering healthy learning environments.

- **Addressing Mental Health Concerns**: As students navigate the complexities of the digital world, educators must be equipped to support their mental health and emotional well-being.

Preparing Educators for the Future

To address these challenges and embrace the opportunities presented by the digital age, educational institutions must invest in the professional development of educators. This includes:

- **Continuous Training**: Providing teachers with regular training sessions on emerging technologies, pedagogical strategies, and digital citizenship education.

- **Collaborative Learning Communities**: Encouraging educators to collaborate and share best practices, fostering a culture of innovation and continuous improvement.

- **Incorporating Student Voice**: Involving students in decision-making processes related to digital education initiatives, ensuring that their perspectives and needs are considered.

Conclusion

The future of education in the digital age presents both exciting opportunities and significant challenges. By embracing personalised learning, blended environments, gamification, SEL, and digital citizenship education, educators can prepare students for success in an increasingly interconnected world. As we move forward, it is essential to prioritise the development of teachers and students alike, ensuring that we create equitable and empowering educational experiences for all. In the next chapter, we will discuss **the importance of building resilient digital communities**, exploring how educators, parents, and students can work together to create a supportive environment for learning in the digital age.

Chapter 16: Building Resilient Digital Communities

Understanding Resilience in Digital Spaces

In an increasingly digital world, resilience refers to the ability of individuals and communities to adapt to challenges, recover from setbacks, and maintain a positive online environment. Building resilient digital communities is crucial for fostering safe, supportive, and engaging learning experiences. This chapter explores the components of resilience in digital spaces, the role of educators in cultivating these communities, and strategies for promoting resilience among students and parents.

1. Components of Resilient Digital Communities

Resilient digital communities share several key characteristics that enable them to thrive in the face of adversity:

- **Supportive Networks**: Strong connections among students, educators, and parents create a sense of belonging and trust. Supportive networks provide emotional and practical assistance, helping individuals navigate challenges.

- **Open Communication**: Transparent and honest communication is vital for building trust and addressing concerns. Communities that encourage open dialogue foster collaboration and collective problem-solving.

- **Adaptability**: Resilient communities can adapt to changing circumstances and challenges. This flexibility allows them to respond effectively to new threats, such as cyberbullying or misinformation.

- **Empowerment**: Empowering individuals within the community to take ownership of their digital experiences fosters a sense of agency. When students feel confident in their ability to navigate online spaces, they are more likely to contribute positively to the community.

2. The Role of Educators in Fostering Resilience

Educators play a crucial role in building resilient digital communities. They can take the following steps to cultivate resilience among students:

- **Model Positive Digital Behaviour**: Educators should demonstrate respectful and responsible online behaviour. By modelling good practices, they set a standard for students to follow.

- **Create Safe Spaces for Discussion**: Establishing a safe environment for students to discuss their online experiences promotes open communication. Educators can facilitate discussions on digital challenges, allowing students to share their concerns and seek support.

- **Teach Coping Strategies**: Educators can equip students with coping strategies to handle online challenges, such as cyberbullying or negative feedback. Teaching resilience skills helps students manage stress and recover from setbacks.

- **Encourage Peer Support**: Fostering a culture of peer support encourages students to help one another navigate challenges. Educators can create initiatives, such as mentorship programmes, where older students support younger peers.

3. Involving Parents in Resilience-Building Efforts

Parents play a vital role in their children's digital experiences and can contribute to building resilient digital communities by:

- **Engaging in Open Conversations**: Encouraging parents to discuss their children's online activities helps establish trust and understanding. Open communication enables parents to address concerns and provide guidance.

- **Participating in Workshops**: Organising workshops for parents on digital literacy, online safety, and social media etiquette empowers them to support their children in navigating digital spaces.

- **Promoting Healthy Screen Time**: Parents can encourage balanced screen time by setting limits and promoting offline activities. Helping children develop a healthy relationship with technology is essential for resilience.

4. Strategies for Promoting Resilience Among Students

Educators and parents can implement various strategies to promote resilience among students:

- **Social-Emotional Learning (SEL)**: Integrating SEL programmes into the curriculum helps students develop emotional intelligence, coping skills, and interpersonal relationships. These skills are essential for navigating digital challenges.

- **Digital Citizenship Education**: Teaching digital citizenship empowers students to make informed decisions, engage positively in online spaces, and advocate for themselves and others.

- **Encouraging Critical Thinking**: Fostering critical thinking skills helps students evaluate online content, recognise bias, and make informed decisions. This skill is essential for navigating misinformation and understanding the digital landscape.

- **Celebrating Successes**: Recognising and celebrating students' achievements, both online and offline, builds confidence and reinforces a positive sense of identity. Acknowledging progress fosters a growth mindset and encourages resilience.

5. Creating a Culture of Inclusion and Diversity

Resilient digital communities value diversity and promote inclusion. To create a culture of inclusion, educators and parents can:

- **Celebrate Diversity**: Acknowledge and celebrate the diverse backgrounds and experiences of students. Incorporating diverse perspectives into the curriculum fosters empathy and understanding.

- **Encourage Collaboration**: Facilitate collaborative projects that bring together students from different backgrounds. Collaborative learning experiences promote teamwork and expose students to diverse viewpoints.

- **Address Discrimination**: Actively combat discrimination and bullying within the community. Educators should create policies and practices that promote equality and inclusivity, ensuring all students feel valued.

Conclusion

Building resilient digital communities is essential for fostering positive online experiences for students and educators alike. By promoting supportive networks, open communication, adaptability, and empowerment, educators can create an environment where students thrive. Involving parents in these efforts further strengthens the community and helps students navigate the digital landscape confidently. In the next chapter, we will explore **the importance of collaboration among educators, students, and parents** in creating a holistic approach to digital literacy and responsibility.

Chapter 17: Collaborative Approaches to Digital Literacy Education

Understanding Collaboration in Digital Literacy

Collaboration in digital literacy education involves the active participation of educators, students, parents, and the broader community to create an inclusive and effective learning environment. By working together, these stakeholders can enhance digital literacy, promote responsible online behaviour, and foster a culture of empathy and respect. This chapter explores the importance of collaboration, effective strategies for engaging all stakeholders, and the potential benefits of a collective approach to digital literacy education.

1. The Importance of Collaboration

Collaborative approaches to digital literacy education are essential for several reasons:

- **Shared Responsibility**: Digital literacy is a collective responsibility. By involving all stakeholders, the educational community can ensure a consistent and comprehensive approach to teaching digital skills.

- **Diverse Perspectives**: Collaboration brings together diverse perspectives and expertise. Each stakeholder—educators, students, parents, and community members—offers unique insights that enrich the learning experience.

- **Enhanced Engagement**: When students see their parents and educators working together, they are more likely to engage meaningfully with digital literacy education. Collaboration fosters a sense of community and support.

- **Addressing Digital Challenges**: Collaborative efforts can effectively address the challenges posed by the digital landscape, such as cyberbullying, misinformation, and privacy concerns. Together, stakeholders can develop strategies and resources to combat these issues.

2. Strategies for Engaging Stakeholders

To effectively promote collaboration in digital literacy education, the following strategies can be employed:

- **Parent Workshops and Information Sessions**: Organising workshops for parents to educate them about digital literacy, online safety, and social media etiquette helps them support their children's learning. Providing resources and practical tips empowers parents to engage in their children's digital education.

- **Student-Led Initiatives**: Encouraging students to take the lead in initiatives related to digital literacy fosters ownership and responsibility. For instance, students can organise digital literacy fairs, peer tutoring programmes, or online safety campaigns that promote awareness and engagement within the community.

- **Teacher Collaboration**: Educators should collaborate across disciplines to integrate digital literacy into various subjects. By working together, teachers can develop interdisciplinary lessons that highlight the importance of digital skills in different contexts.

- **Community Partnerships**: Building partnerships with local organisations, businesses, and non-profits can provide additional resources and expertise. Collaborating with community stakeholders can enrich the educational experience and offer students real-world insights into digital literacy.

3. Creating a Supportive Learning Environment

For collaboration to be effective, a supportive learning environment must be established:

- **Open Communication Channels**: Establishing open lines of communication among all stakeholders encourages dialogue and feedback. Regular meetings, newsletters, and online forums can facilitate ongoing discussions about digital literacy initiatives.

- **Fostering Trust**: Building trust among educators, students, and parents is essential for successful collaboration. Creating a culture of respect, empathy, and transparency helps strengthen relationships within the educational community.

- **Celebrating Collaborative Achievements**: Recognising and celebrating collaborative efforts fosters a sense of accomplishment and encourages continued participation. Celebrating successes, whether big or small, reinforces the value of working together.

4. Evaluating Collaborative Efforts

To ensure the effectiveness of collaborative approaches to digital literacy education, it is essential to evaluate progress regularly:

- **Setting Clear Goals**: Establish clear objectives for collaborative initiatives and regularly assess progress towards these goals. Involving all stakeholders in goal-setting promotes accountability and ownership.

- **Collecting Feedback**: Gather feedback from students, parents, and educators to identify strengths and areas for improvement. Surveys, focus groups, and open forums can provide valuable insights into the effectiveness of collaborative efforts.

- **Adjusting Strategies**: Use evaluation results to adjust strategies and approaches as needed. Flexibility and adaptability are key to ensuring that collaborative initiatives remain relevant and effective.

5. The Role of Technology in Collaboration

Technology can play a crucial role in facilitating collaboration among stakeholders:

- **Online Collaboration Tools**: Utilising online platforms such as Google Classroom, Microsoft Teams, or Slack can enhance communication and collaboration among educators, students, and parents. These tools allow for real-time sharing of resources, feedback, and ideas.

- **Virtual Meetings and Webinars**: Hosting virtual meetings and webinars enables broader participation from parents and community members who may not be able to attend in-person events. Online events can increase accessibility and engagement.

- **Social Media for Community Building**: Creating dedicated social media groups or forums can foster a sense of community among stakeholders. These platforms can facilitate discussions, share resources, and provide a space for support and collaboration.

Conclusion

Collaborative approaches to digital literacy education are vital for creating a well-rounded learning experience that empowers students to navigate the digital world responsibly. By engaging all stakeholders—educators, students, parents, and the community—educators can cultivate a culture of shared responsibility and support. In the next chapter, we will examine **how to create comprehensive digital literacy programmes that address the unique needs of students in diverse educational settings**.

Chapter 18: Developing Comprehensive Digital Literacy Programmes

1. The Importance of Comprehensive Digital Literacy Education

In today's interconnected world, digital literacy is not just a supplementary skill but a foundational one. It encompasses much more than the ability to use devices; it involves critical thinking, ethical use of digital tools, understanding the socio-technical landscape, and fostering responsible online behaviours. Comprehensive digital literacy programmes prepare students to navigate the complexities of the digital age, making informed decisions and participating meaningfully in digital environments.

2. Key Components of a Digital Literacy Programme

A comprehensive digital literacy programme should address multiple aspects of digital engagement, preparing students for personal, academic, and professional success. The following are key components to include:

- **Digital Competency**: Teaching technical skills such as using software, hardware, and online platforms is fundamental. Students should become proficient in using various digital tools to complete tasks, solve problems, and communicate effectively.

- **Online Safety and Privacy**: Understanding how to protect personal information, manage privacy settings, and recognise potential online threats such as phishing, cyberbullying, and identity theft is crucial. Educators must emphasise digital hygiene practices that help students stay secure online.

- **Ethical Digital Citizenship**: A comprehensive programme should instil ethical considerations, such as respecting intellectual property, understanding copyright laws, and recognising the importance of respectful online communication. This also includes educating students on the impact of their digital footprint.

- **Media Literacy**: In an age where misinformation and fake news proliferate, teaching students how to critically assess the credibility of online content is essential. This includes identifying biases, recognising credible sources, and understanding the role of algorithms in shaping information exposure.

- **Digital Etiquette**: Good online manners, appropriate communication in digital spaces, and understanding context and tone in written interactions should be taught. Emphasising empathy and responsible behaviour online helps create a respectful and inclusive digital environment.

- **Collaboration and Creation**: Encouraging students to collaborate on digital platforms and create original content fosters creativity and teamwork. Digital literacy is not just about consumption but also about producing and sharing knowledge in a responsible way.

3. Customising Programmes for Different Educational Levels

Digital literacy programmes must be tailored to suit the developmental stages and specific needs of different educational levels. Below are some strategies for customising digital literacy education:

- **Primary Education**: At this stage, programmes should focus on basic digital skills, such as navigating the internet safely, understanding simple privacy settings, and recognising the importance of online kindness and empathy. Interactive and engaging content is key to maintaining the interest of younger students.

- **Secondary Education**: For older students, programmes should become more advanced, focusing on critical thinking skills, deeper media literacy, and the ethical dimensions of online behaviour. Students should also be taught how to use more sophisticated digital tools, such as presentation software, coding, or digital collaboration platforms.

- **Higher Education**: Digital literacy programmes at the tertiary level should focus on preparing students for the professional world. This includes advanced research skills, understanding the legal implications of online content, creating a professional online presence, and collaborating effectively in digital environments. Integrating digital literacy into various academic disciplines can help students apply these skills in their chosen fields.

4. Integrating Digital Literacy into the Curriculum

Rather than treating digital literacy as a standalone subject, it should be embedded into all areas of the curriculum. This cross-disciplinary approach ensures that digital literacy skills are applied in context, making them more relevant and impactful.

- **STEM Subjects**: Digital literacy is naturally aligned with STEM education. Integrating coding, data analysis, and digital project-based learning in science, technology, engineering, and mathematics enhances students' technical proficiency and problem-solving abilities.

- **Humanities and Social Sciences**: Digital literacy in these subjects might involve media analysis, digital research techniques, or understanding the social impact of digital technology. It also provides opportunities to explore ethical questions related to the digital world.

- **Arts and Creative Subjects**: Teaching digital creation tools—such as video editing software, digital illustration, or social media platforms—encourages students to express themselves and explore digital culture creatively. Understanding the interplay between digital media and traditional artistic forms is increasingly important in today's creative industries.

5. Training Educators to Teach Digital Literacy

Effective digital literacy education depends on the proficiency and confidence of educators. Teachers must be equipped with the necessary skills and understanding to teach digital literacy meaningfully. Key strategies for educator training include:

- **Ongoing Professional Development**: Schools and educational institutions should offer regular training sessions for educators, ensuring they stay updated on the latest digital tools, trends, and challenges. Workshops, seminars, and certification courses can provide educators with practical skills they can apply in the classroom.

- **Collaboration and Knowledge Sharing**: Educators should be encouraged to collaborate and share best practices in teaching digital literacy. Online forums, peer review sessions, and professional networks can facilitate knowledge exchange.

- **Resources and Tools for Educators**: Providing educators with access to digital literacy curricula, lesson plans, and assessment tools ensures they have the resources needed to implement effective programmes. Institutions should invest in digital platforms and resources that support teaching and learning.

6. Assessing Digital Literacy

Measuring digital literacy is essential for understanding student progress and the effectiveness of programmes. Assessments can be conducted in several ways:

- **Formative Assessments**: These include quizzes, practical projects, and peer assessments that provide continuous feedback. This approach allows educators to identify areas where students need more support.

- **Digital Portfolios**: Encouraging students to create digital portfolios of their work allows them to demonstrate their digital literacy skills over time. These portfolios can showcase technical proficiency, creativity, and critical thinking.

- **Competency-Based Assessments**: Rather than focusing solely on test results, assessments can be designed to evaluate students' ability to apply digital literacy skills in real-world scenarios. For example, students might be tasked with evaluating the credibility of a news article or creating a digital campaign on a social issue.

7. The Future of Digital Literacy Education

As technology continues to evolve, so too will the skills required for digital literacy. Preparing students for the future means keeping digital literacy programmes dynamic and adaptable. Educators should remain agile, continuously updating content to reflect the latest technological trends and challenges.

Conclusion

Developing comprehensive digital literacy programmes is critical for preparing students to navigate the digital landscape effectively and responsibly. By embedding digital literacy into the curriculum, training educators, and assessing progress, educational institutions can equip the next generation with the skills needed to thrive in the digital age. The next chapter will explore **how to integrate ethical considerations into digital literacy programmes**, ensuring that students not only become skilled digital citizens but also responsible and ethical participants in the online world.

Chapter 19: Integrating Ethical Considerations into Digital Literacy Programmes

1. The Role of Ethics in Digital Literacy

As students become increasingly immersed in digital environments, teaching them not just how to use digital tools but how to use them ethically is paramount. Digital literacy programmes should include a strong ethical component to ensure that students understand the moral implications of their online behaviour. This includes respecting intellectual property, understanding privacy rights, avoiding cyberbullying, and recognising the broader societal impacts of technology.

Ethics in digital literacy education goes beyond basic online etiquette—it encompasses responsible content creation, respect for diversity, the ethical use of information, and understanding the consequences of digital actions.

2. Ethical Issues in the Digital World

Educators must address several key ethical issues in digital literacy, preparing students to make informed and principled decisions online. These include:

- **Digital Rights and Privacy**: As students engage with various digital platforms, they need to understand their rights concerning data protection and privacy. Ethical discussions should focus on how personal data is collected, used, and potentially exploited by companies, as well as the individual's responsibility to protect their own and others' personal information.

- **Intellectual Property and Copyright**: In an age of information sharing, students need to understand what constitutes plagiarism and intellectual property theft. Ethical digital literacy programmes should teach students the importance of citing sources, using content legally, and respecting creators' rights, while also discussing fair use and open access resources.

- **Cyberbullying and Online Harassment**: One of the most pressing ethical concerns in digital spaces is the rise of cyberbullying and harassment. Digital literacy programmes must address the responsibility individuals have to behave respectfully online, the consequences of cyberbullying, and how students can protect themselves and others from harassment.

- **Misinformation and Fake News**: The spread of false information online has significant ethical implications, especially when it comes to public decision-making. Teaching students how to critically evaluate information and avoid spreading false or misleading content is a key ethical component of digital literacy.

- **Algorithmic Bias**: Many digital platforms use algorithms to determine what content users see, and these algorithms can often reinforce biases. Students should be educated on the ethical implications of algorithmic bias and the responsibility of both users and creators to address these issues.

3. Teaching Ethical Digital Citizenship

Incorporating ethics into digital literacy means educating students to be responsible digital citizens who understand their role in creating a positive online culture. Ethical digital citizenship involves several key principles:

- **Accountability for Online Actions**: Students must learn that their actions online can have real-world consequences. This includes teaching them to be accountable for their behaviour in digital spaces, whether it's contributing to constructive discussions or avoiding harmful actions like trolling or doxxing.

- **Respect for Diversity**: The internet is a global space where people from various cultures, backgrounds, and belief systems interact. Ethical digital literacy should emphasise the importance of respecting diverse perspectives, fostering tolerance, and avoiding discriminatory or harmful language.

- **Critical Reflection on Digital Practices**: Ethical digital citizens should regularly reflect on their own use of technology. Students should be encouraged to consider how their digital behaviours affect others and whether their actions align with their values and those of their communities.

4. Strategies for Embedding Ethics in Digital Literacy Programmes

Embedding ethics into digital literacy education requires careful planning and the integration of practical activities that promote ethical awareness. Some effective strategies include:

- **Case Studies and Scenarios**: Presenting students with real-life examples of ethical dilemmas in digital spaces allows them to engage in critical thinking and problem-solving. Case studies can cover issues such as data breaches, online harassment, or intellectual property disputes, giving students a chance to consider different perspectives and outcomes.

- **Ethical Debates and Discussions**: Classroom discussions and debates on controversial digital topics can help students explore ethical considerations more deeply. For example, educators might facilitate discussions on the ethics of surveillance technology, the impact of social media algorithms, or the balance between free speech and responsible online communication.

- **Role-Playing Exercises**: Role-playing can be an effective way to help students understand the impact of their digital actions on others. For example, students could role-play a scenario where one individual shares someone else's personal information without consent, exploring the ethical implications from both perspectives.

- **Collaborative Projects on Digital Ethics**: Group projects that require students to research and present on specific ethical issues in the digital world encourage collaboration and the sharing of diverse viewpoints. These projects can cover a range of topics, such as digital privacy laws, the environmental impact of technology, or the ethics of artificial intelligence.

5. Challenges in Teaching Digital Ethics

While teaching digital ethics is essential, there are several challenges that educators may face in integrating these topics into digital literacy programmes:

- **Evolving Technology**: As technology rapidly changes, new ethical challenges continually emerge. Educators must stay up-to-date with the latest developments in digital ethics, which requires ongoing professional development and adaptability.

- **Cultural and Personal Beliefs**: Ethical perspectives can vary based on cultural backgrounds and personal beliefs. This can make it challenging to create a digital literacy curriculum that resonates with all students. Educators must be sensitive to these differences while promoting universal ethical principles, such as respect and accountability.

- **Balancing Ethics with Practical Skills**: Digital literacy programmes often need to cover a wide range of technical skills and competencies, leaving limited time for in-depth discussions on ethics. Finding the right balance between teaching practical skills and fostering ethical awareness is crucial for a well-rounded programme.

6. The Role of Educators in Promoting Digital Ethics

Educators play a pivotal role in modelling ethical behaviour and guiding students through the complex moral landscape of the digital world. Some key responsibilities include:

- **Modelling Ethical Behaviour**: Educators should lead by example, demonstrating ethical online practices in their own digital interactions. This includes citing sources, respecting privacy, and maintaining professionalism in online communication.

- **Creating a Safe and Respectful Digital Environment**: In both physical and virtual classrooms, educators should create a culture of respect and inclusivity. This involves setting clear expectations for online conduct and addressing any incidents of cyberbullying or inappropriate behaviour swiftly and effectively.

- **Facilitating Open Dialogue**: Educators should encourage students to ask questions and share their perspectives on ethical issues in digital spaces. By fostering an open, non-judgmental dialogue, educators can help students develop a deeper understanding of the ethical complexities they will face online.

7. Evaluating Ethical Understanding in Digital Literacy Programmes

Assessing students' ethical understanding is an essential component of digital literacy education. However, measuring ethical knowledge and behaviour can be challenging. Some methods for evaluation include:

- **Reflective Essays and Journals**: Encouraging students to reflect on their digital behaviour and ethical considerations in writing can provide valuable insights into their understanding. Essays or journals that prompt students to analyse ethical scenarios or discuss their own digital experiences can be effective assessment tools.

- **Peer Reviews and Group Discussions**: Peer reviews and group discussions allow students to engage with different perspectives and consider how their peers interpret ethical issues. Evaluating students based on their participation and ability to articulate ethical concepts can help educators gauge their level of understanding.

- **Scenario-Based Assessments**: Presenting students with hypothetical ethical dilemmas and asking them to suggest solutions can be an effective way to assess their critical thinking and ethical reasoning skills.

Conclusion

Integrating ethical considerations into digital literacy programmes is essential for developing responsible, thoughtful digital citizens who can navigate the complexities of the online world with integrity. By equipping students with the skills to critically evaluate their actions and make informed decisions, educators play a crucial role in shaping the future of ethical digital engagement. The following chapter will explore **how to develop digital literacy curricula that foster collaboration and community-building**, ensuring that students not only become proficient digital users but also positive contributors to the online world.

Chapter 20: Developing Collaborative Digital Literacy Curricula

1. The Importance of Collaboration in Digital Literacy

As the digital landscape becomes more interconnected, collaborative skills are essential for effective participation in online communities and professional environments. Digital literacy curricula should not only focus on individual competencies but also foster collaborative abilities, such as teamwork, communication, and shared problem-solving. By incorporating collaborative learning into digital literacy education, students can better navigate the cooperative nature of the digital world.

Collaboration in digital spaces includes working on shared documents, engaging in group discussions, and contributing to online communities. Educators must teach students how to collaborate effectively, manage digital teamwork, and resolve conflicts that may arise in collaborative online settings.

2. Digital Tools for Collaboration

To help students thrive in collaborative digital environments, it's crucial to familiarise them with the tools that facilitate online teamwork. These include:

- **Cloud-Based Platforms**: Tools like Google Drive, Microsoft OneDrive, and Dropbox allow students to create, share, and edit documents in real-time, supporting collaboration across various devices.

- **Communication and Project Management Tools**: Platforms like Slack, Microsoft Teams, and Trello enable students to organise projects, assign tasks, and communicate efficiently in both academic and professional settings.

- **Collaborative Editing Tools**: Programmes like Google Docs and Microsoft Word's collaborative mode allow multiple users to edit and comment on the same document simultaneously, fostering real-time cooperation.

- **Social Media for Academic Collaboration**: Platforms such as LinkedIn and specialised online communities can be valuable for group learning, networking, and collaboration on academic and professional projects.

Teaching students how to use these tools effectively is a key component of any digital literacy curriculum.

3. Building Teamwork Skills in Digital Literacy Education

While digital tools facilitate collaboration, developing the soft skills necessary for effective teamwork is equally important. These skills include:

- **Clear Communication**: Students must learn how to communicate clearly and professionally in online environments. Misunderstandings often arise in digital interactions due to the lack of visual cues and tone, making it critical for students to practise concise, respectful communication.

- **Conflict Resolution**: In collaborative environments, disagreements are inevitable. Educators must teach students how to handle conflicts constructively, ensuring that they can resolve differences without damaging team cohesion.

- **Time Management**: Managing time and meeting deadlines are critical in collaborative projects, especially when working in virtual teams where members may be in different locations or time zones. Time management tools and strategies should be introduced as part of collaborative education.

- **Sharing Responsibilities**: Effective collaboration requires equitable division of tasks. Students should be taught how to delegate responsibilities, ensuring that all members contribute fairly to the group's success.

4. Collaborative Learning Models in Digital Literacy

Several educational models emphasise collaboration as a core component of learning. These models can be adapted to digital literacy curricula:

- **Project-Based Learning (PBL)**: In PBL, students work together on complex projects that require them to apply their digital skills in real-world scenarios. For example, students might collaborate on designing a website, developing a digital marketing campaign, or producing multimedia content. PBL fosters teamwork, problem-solving, and critical thinking, all of which are vital in the digital age.

- **Peer Learning**: Peer learning allows students to learn from each other's expertise. In digital literacy, this might involve students with advanced skills in certain areas (such as coding, video production, or social media analytics) teaching their peers, thereby reinforcing their own knowledge while building a collaborative learning environment.

- **Collaborative Problem-Solving**: This model encourages students to work together to solve complex digital problems, such as analysing fake news or devising strategies to improve digital security. Collaborative problem-solving not only enhances critical thinking skills but also teaches students to value diverse perspectives.

5. Promoting Global Collaboration in Digital Literacy

The internet enables collaboration on a global scale, and students should be encouraged to engage with peers and professionals worldwide. Global collaboration offers several educational benefits:

- **Cultural Exchange and Learning**: Collaborating with individuals from different countries and cultures helps students develop a broader worldview, teaching them to appreciate diverse perspectives and communication styles.

- **International Project Partnerships**: Students can work on collaborative projects with peers in other countries, gaining insights into how digital literacy is applied in different cultural and technological contexts. For instance, a project might involve students from multiple countries working together to create a digital media campaign addressing a global issue like climate change or digital privacy.

- **Leveraging Global Expertise**: Educators can connect students with international experts through webinars, virtual conferences, or social media platforms. These collaborations provide students with unique opportunities to learn from professionals who bring global expertise in areas like cybersecurity, digital marketing, or media literacy.

6. Addressing Challenges in Collaborative Digital Learning

While collaborative digital learning has many benefits, it also presents several challenges that educators need to address:

- **Unequal Participation**: In group projects, some students may take on more work than others, leading to resentment and an imbalance in contribution. Educators can mitigate this by setting clear expectations for group work and regularly checking in with students to ensure that tasks are distributed fairly.

- **Technological Barriers**: Not all students may have access to the same technological tools or reliable internet connections, which can hinder collaboration. Schools and institutions must ensure that all students have equal access to the necessary technology to fully participate in digital literacy programmes.

- **Time Zone Differences**: In global collaborations, coordinating across time zones can be difficult. Educators should teach students how to manage these challenges by using tools like scheduling software and encouraging flexibility in planning collaborative sessions.

- **Language Barriers**: In international collaborations, language differences may pose challenges to effective communication. Encouraging students to use clear, simple language and providing translation tools can help bridge these gaps.

7. Practical Exercises for Collaborative Digital Literacy

To ensure students effectively apply collaborative skills in digital literacy, educators can incorporate the following practical exercises:

- **Group Research Projects**: Assign students to work in teams to research a digital issue, such as the impact of social media algorithms or the ethical use of artificial intelligence. Teams should present their findings through a collaborative digital presentation.

- **Online Discussion Forums**: Set up virtual discussion forums where students must respond to each other's ideas and collaborate on solving digital literacy-related challenges. This fosters both critical thinking and collaboration in a controlled, academic setting.

- **Collaborative Content Creation**: Encourage students to work together on creating digital content, such as videos, podcasts, or blog posts. This exercise teaches students to combine their technical skills with creative collaboration.

8. Assessing Collaboration in Digital Literacy

Evaluating students' collaborative skills can be challenging, but there are several methods to ensure fair and comprehensive assessment:

- **Self and Peer Assessments**: Encourage students to assess their own contributions as well as their peers'. This helps identify strengths and areas for improvement in teamwork.

- **Process-Based Evaluation**: Instead of focusing solely on the final product, assess students based on how they approached collaboration, including how they divided tasks, resolved conflicts, and communicated.

- **Collaborative Portfolios**: Have students create a digital portfolio showcasing their collaborative projects. This not only serves as an assessment tool but also provides students with a tangible record of their collaborative achievements.

Conclusion

Collaboration is a fundamental skill in the digital world, and it's essential that digital literacy curricula reflect this reality. By fostering effective teamwork, promoting global collaboration, and teaching students how to use digital tools for collective problem-solving, educators can prepare students to thrive in both academic and professional environments. The following chapter will focus on **the role of digital literacy in lifelong learning**, exploring how individuals can continue to adapt and grow in an ever-changing digital landscape.

Chapter 21: The Role of Digital Literacy in Lifelong Learning

1. Understanding Lifelong Learning in the Digital Age

Lifelong learning refers to the ongoing, voluntary pursuit of knowledge for both personal and professional development. In today's fast-paced digital world, this concept is more relevant than ever. The digital age has transformed how individuals access information, acquire new skills, and stay competitive in an evolving job market.

Digital literacy is central to lifelong learning, as it equips individuals with the ability to navigate the vast array of online resources, tools, and technologies necessary for continuous learning. Educators must not only instil digital literacy skills in students but also foster a mindset that values lifelong learning in an increasingly digital environment.

2. Why Digital Literacy Is Crucial for Lifelong Learning

The digital world is constantly evolving, with new platforms, technologies, and information appearing every day. As such, digital literacy is not a one-time skill but an ongoing process of adaptation and refinement. Lifelong learners need to stay digitally literate to:

- **Stay Competitive in the Job Market**: As automation, artificial intelligence (AI), and digital tools become more prevalent, individuals must continue updating their digital skills to remain employable and adaptable to new roles and industries.

- **Access Information and Education**: The internet offers unprecedented access to educational resources, from online courses and webinars to tutorials and open-access journals. Without strong digital literacy skills, individuals may struggle to locate, evaluate, and apply these resources effectively.

- **Adapt to New Technologies**: As new tools, platforms, and applications emerge, individuals need to continuously update their knowledge of how to use them. Digital literacy ensures that lifelong learners can remain proficient and confident in their ability to adapt to technological changes.

- **Participate in Digital Communities**: Beyond personal growth, digital literacy enables individuals to engage meaningfully in online communities, whether for professional networking, academic collaboration, or personal interests.

3. Lifelong Learning Models in the Digital Era

Various models of lifelong learning can be integrated into digital literacy education, each designed to foster ongoing intellectual and skill development. These models include:

- **Self-Directed Learning**: This model encourages individuals to take initiative in their learning journey by identifying their needs, setting goals, and finding resources independently. Digital literacy is key to navigating online platforms, locating relevant content, and assessing the quality of information.

- **Blended Learning**: Combining traditional classroom instruction with digital tools, blended learning allows learners to access a mix of in-person and online content. Lifelong learners use digital platforms to supplement their education, attend virtual classes, and engage in self-paced learning.

- **Microlearning**: Digital literacy can support microlearning, where individuals engage in short, focused learning experiences via digital platforms. Microlearning tools like mobile apps, videos, and podcasts are effective for teaching specific skills or knowledge in small doses, making it easier for lifelong learners to fit education into their daily routines.

- **Massive Open Online Courses (MOOCs)**: Platforms like Coursera, edX, and FutureLearn provide access to a wide range of courses from top universities and institutions. These courses allow learners to develop digital literacy by engaging with a variety of subjects at their own pace.

4. Digital Tools Supporting Lifelong Learning

Numerous digital tools are available to facilitate lifelong learning. Educators should introduce students to these tools and help them develop strategies for using them effectively:

- **Learning Management Systems (LMS)**: Tools like Canvas, Moodle, and Blackboard provide lifelong learners with structured online courses, progress tracking, and forums for peer interaction.

- **Educational Platforms**: Websites such as Khan Academy, LinkedIn Learning, and Skillshare offer tutorials and courses in a wide range of subjects. These platforms often provide certificates that learners can add to their portfolios or CVs.

- **Mobile Learning Apps**: Apps like Duolingo, Quizlet, and Coursera allow learners to access education from their smartphones, making lifelong learning more accessible and flexible.

- **E-Libraries and Open Access Resources**: Digital libraries, such as Google Scholar and JSTOR, provide access to research articles, journals, and academic papers, enabling learners to pursue in-depth study of any subject.

5. Teaching Digital Literacy as a Lifelong Skill

Digital literacy should not be viewed as a static set of competencies but rather as a dynamic and evolving skillset. To foster lifelong learning, educators must focus on teaching students how to:

- **Adapt to Technological Changes**: Ensure that students understand the need to continuously update their digital skills as technology evolves. Encourage them to explore new tools and platforms proactively and to seek out professional development opportunities.

- **Use Online Resources for Continuous Learning**: Teach students how to locate reliable online courses, tutorials, and learning communities to support their ongoing education. Introduce them to key platforms and teach them how to evaluate the quality of available resources.

- **Practice Critical Thinking and Digital Literacy Together**: Critical thinking is a core aspect of digital literacy and lifelong learning. Equip students with the ability to critically assess information, especially in an era of misinformation and rapidly changing digital environments.

6. The Role of Lifelong Learning in Professional Development

In professional settings, digital literacy is often directly linked to career advancement and long-term success. Individuals who commit to lifelong learning tend to experience:

- **Improved Job Opportunities**: Professionals with advanced digital skills are more competitive in the job market. Employers value workers who can adapt to new tools, platforms, and processes.

- **Increased Confidence and Flexibility**: Lifelong learners are more confident in their ability to navigate changes in their industry. They are often better equipped to take on new responsibilities and challenges.

- **Networking and Collaboration**: Professionals who engage in lifelong learning frequently participate in online learning communities and forums. This networking can lead to new job opportunities and collaborative projects.

7. Encouraging Lifelong Learning in Educational Settings

To prepare students for lifelong learning, educational institutions can implement strategies such as:

- **Promoting a Growth Mindset**: Encourage students to view learning as a lifelong process. Emphasise the importance of curiosity, adaptability, and perseverance in their academic and professional journeys.

- **Incorporating Lifelong Learning Skills into the Curriculum**: Educators should include modules that teach students how to seek out new learning opportunities, adapt to technological changes, and engage in self-directed education.

- **Creating Pathways for Continuous Learning**: Provide students with access to online learning platforms and resources, helping them to continue their education after they leave formal schooling.

Conclusion

In an ever-changing digital world, lifelong learning is not just a luxury but a necessity. By mastering digital literacy and adopting a mindset of continuous growth, individuals can stay informed, adapt to new technologies, and thrive in both personal and professional environments. Educators play a crucial role in preparing students to embrace lifelong learning, ensuring they remain competent and confident in their ability to navigate the digital landscape for years to come. The final chapter will focus on **empowering educators to lead in the digital literacy revolution**, offering practical advice on how to champion digital learning initiatives within their institutions and communities.

Chapter 22: Empowering Educators to Lead the Digital Literacy Revolution

1. The Role of Educators in Shaping Digital Competence

Educators have a unique responsibility to shape the digital competence of their students, equipping them with the skills necessary to thrive in a world dominated by digital technologies. As leaders in the digital literacy revolution, educators must go beyond traditional teaching methods and adopt strategies that reflect the realities of a digital-first world. This involves integrating digital tools into the classroom, developing robust digital literacy curricula, and cultivating an environment where digital etiquette, empathy, and critical thinking are embedded into everyday learning.

2. Educators as Digital Literacy Advocates

Educators must position themselves as advocates for digital literacy within their schools, institutions, and communities. Advocacy involves:

- **Raising Awareness**: Helping students, parents, and colleagues understand the importance of digital literacy, particularly in a world where misinformation and online risks are prevalent.

- **Staying Informed**: Digital literacy is constantly evolving. Educators must stay up to date with new technologies, social media trends, and emerging digital platforms to ensure that their teaching remains relevant.

- **Collaborating with Stakeholders**: Work with fellow educators, school administrators, and policymakers to integrate digital literacy into educational policies and standards. Collaborations with external organisations, such as tech companies or educational nonprofits, can also support the development of high-quality digital literacy programs.

- **Modelling Good Digital Practice**: Educators should lead by example, showcasing good digital etiquette, effective use of technology, and critical evaluation of online resources in their personal and professional online behaviour.

3. Developing a Digital Literacy Curriculum

Creating a robust digital literacy curriculum involves careful planning and alignment with broader educational objectives. Key components include:

- **Foundational Digital Skills**: Teaching students the basics of how to use digital tools, from email and internet browsers to more complex software and platforms. It also includes helping them understand how digital systems work, including data processing, algorithms, and cloud storage.

- **Digital Ethics and Citizenship**: Introducing topics such as digital etiquette, online responsibility, privacy, and the ethical use of technology. Students should understand the long-term consequences of their digital actions, including their digital footprint and the potential for cyberbullying.

- **Critical Thinking and Media Literacy**: Educators should integrate critical thinking skills that help students evaluate online content. This includes recognising bias, identifying credible sources, and understanding the mechanisms behind digital manipulation (e.g., fake news, deepfakes).

- **Social Media and Communication**: As social media is central to modern communication, it is vital to teach students how to navigate these platforms responsibly, maintain privacy, and communicate clearly and respectfully online.

- **Cybersecurity Awareness**: Ensuring that students understand the basics of online safety, including how to protect themselves from phishing, malware, and identity theft, and the importance of strong password management.

4. Implementing Digital Literacy in Educational Settings

Educators need practical strategies to incorporate digital literacy into everyday teaching. These include:

- **Project-Based Learning**: Assign projects that require students to engage with digital tools and platforms, such as researching online, creating digital content, or evaluating media. This not only enhances digital literacy but also fosters critical thinking and collaboration.

- **Interactive and Engaging Tools**: Use educational technologies that make learning digital literacy more interactive and enjoyable. These can include educational apps, gamified learning experiences, and digital storytelling platforms.

- **Blended Learning Models**: Incorporate a mix of traditional teaching and digital resources, such as e-learning platforms, virtual classrooms, and collaborative online tools like Google Workspace or Microsoft Teams. This allows students to develop digital literacy in a real-world context.

- **Continuous Assessment and Feedback**: Implement ongoing assessments that gauge students' digital literacy progress. This can include quizzes on internet safety, peer reviews of digital projects, or reflective essays on their use of digital tools. Feedback should be constructive, helping students improve their digital competencies.

5. Overcoming Challenges in Teaching Digital Literacy

Educators often face obstacles in integrating digital literacy into their teaching. These can include:

- **Lack of Resources**: Many schools lack the necessary digital infrastructure, such as up-to-date hardware or reliable internet access. To address this, educators can seek grants, partner with tech companies for resources, or explore open-source software and tools that provide free or low-cost alternatives.

- **Teacher Training Gaps**: Some educators may not feel confident in their own digital literacy skills. Schools should offer professional development programs that train teachers on how to use digital tools, integrate technology into their lessons, and stay current with digital trends.

- **Diverse Digital Competency Levels**: Not all students come into the classroom with the same level of digital literacy. Some may have grown up with constant internet access, while others may have limited exposure to technology. Educators need to differentiate their teaching approaches to ensure that all students, regardless of background, develop the necessary digital skills.

6. Creating a Supportive Digital Learning Environment

To foster digital literacy, educators must create a classroom environment where students feel safe and supported in their digital exploration. This includes:

- **Encouraging Curiosity and Experimentation**: Encourage students to explore new digital tools, ask questions about technology, and experiment with different ways of using digital platforms.

- **Promoting Safe Digital Spaces**: Ensure that students are aware of how to use technology responsibly and respectfully. Promote discussions around digital well-being, including the mental health impact of social media, online harassment, and the importance of unplugging.

- **Fostering Collaboration**: Digital literacy is often best learned through collaboration. Encourage students to work together on digital projects, share resources, and support each other in developing new skills.

7. Engaging with Parents and the Wider Community

Educators are not alone in their efforts to teach digital literacy. Engaging with parents and the wider community can create a more holistic approach to digital education. Key strategies include:

- **Parent Workshops and Resources**: Provide workshops that educate parents on digital literacy, online safety, and the role of social media in their children's lives. Offer resources and guides that help them support their children's digital development at home.

- **Community Partnerships**: Collaborate with local businesses, tech companies, and community organisations to provide students with opportunities to engage with digital tools in real-world settings. These partnerships can also help bring in resources and expertise to support digital education.

8. Leading the Digital Literacy Revolution

As digital literacy continues to grow in importance, educators must take a leadership role in ensuring that it becomes a priority in educational institutions. This involves:

- **Advocating for Digital Literacy in Policy**: Work with policymakers and education boards to ensure that digital literacy is included in the national curriculum and that schools are equipped with the resources needed to teach it effectively.

- **Empowering Fellow Educators**: Share knowledge and strategies with other teachers, helping to create a culture of digital literacy within schools. Lead workshops, create digital literacy resource libraries, and mentor colleagues who may need support in integrating digital tools into their teaching.

- **Promoting Digital Literacy as a Lifelong Skill**: Emphasise to students, parents, and colleagues that digital literacy is not a finite skill set but an ongoing process that requires continuous learning and adaptation.

Conclusion: Pioneering the Future of Education

In an increasingly digital world, educators have the power to shape the future by leading the digital literacy revolution. By embracing technology, fostering critical thinking, and advocating for responsible online behaviour, educators can ensure that their students are not only digitally competent but also ethical and empathetic digital citizens. This chapter sets the stage for future discussions on how digital literacy will continue to evolve and the educator's vital role in shaping that future.

www.ingramcontent.com/pod-product-compliance
Lightning Source LLC
LaVergne TN
LVHW081528050326
832903LV00025B/1687